# Meeting the Needs

## of Your Most Able Pupils:

# RELIGIOUS EDUCATION

## Other titles in the series

# Meeting the Needs
## of Your Most Able Pupils:

# RELIGIOUS
# EDUCATION

**Dilwyn Hunt**

Routledge
Taylor & Francis Group

LONDON AND NEW YORK

First published 2007 by
Routledge
2 Park Square, Milton Park, Abingdon, Oxon OX14 4RN

Simultaneously published in the USA and Canada by
Routledge
270 Madison Ave, New York, NY 10016

*Routledge is an imprint of Taylor & Francis, an informa business*

Copyright © Dilwyn Hunt 2007

*British Library Cataloguing in Publication data*
A catalogue record for this book is available from the British Library

*Library of Congress Cataloging in Publication Data*
A catalog record has been requested

ISBN 13: 978 1 84312 278 4 (pbk)
ISBN 13: 978 0 203 93540 8 (ebk)
ISBN 10: 1 84312 278 2 (pbk)
ISBN 10: 0 203 93540 3 (ebk)

Series production editors: Sarah Fish and Andrew Welsh
Typeset by Servis Filmsetting Ltd, Manchester
Printed and bound in Great Britain
by Bell & Bain Ltd, Glasgow

# Contents

# Contributors to the series

## The author

**Dilwyn Hunt** has worked as a specialist RE adviser in Birmingham and Dudley in the West Midlands, and has a wide range of teaching experience. He is currently a school adviser with responsibility for gifted and talented pupils.

## Series editor

**Gwen Goodhew's** many and varied roles within the field of gifted and talented education have included school G&T coordinator, director of Wirral Able Children Centre, Knowsley Excellence in Cities (EiC) G&T coordinator, member of the DfES G&T Advisory Group, teacher trainer and consultant. She has written and edited numerous reports and articles on the subject and co-authored *Providing for Able Children* with Linda Evans.

## Other authors

### Art

**Kim Earle** is a former secondary head of art and design and is currently an able pupils and arts consultant for St Helens. She has been a member of DfES steering groups, is an Artsmark validator, a subject editor for G&TWISE and is a practising designer jeweller and enameller.

### Design and Technology

During the writing of the book **Louise T. Davies** was a part-time subject adviser for design and technology at the QCA (Qualifications and Curriculum Authority), and part of the KS3 National Strategy team for the D&T programme. She has authored over 40 D&T books and award-winning multimedia resources. She is currently deputy chief executive of the Design and Technology Association.

### Geography

**Jane Ferretti** is a lecturer in education at the University of Sheffield working in initial teacher training. Until 2003 she was head of geography at King Edward VII School, Sheffield, a large 11–18 comprehensive, and was also involved in gifted and talented initiatives at the school and with the local authority. Jane has co-authored a number of A level geography textbooks and a GCSE revision book and is one of the editors of *Wideworld* magazine. She is a member of the Geographical Association and a contributor to their journals *Teaching Geography* and *Geography*.

## History

**Steven Barnes** is a former head of history at a secondary school and Secondary Strategy consultant for the School Improvement Service in Lincolnshire. He has written history exemplifications for Assessment for Learning for the Secondary National Strategy. He is now an assistant head with responsibility for teaching and learning for a school in Lincolnshire.

## Mathematics

**Lynne McClure** is an independent consultant in the field of mathematics education and G&T. She works with teachers and students in schools all over the UK and abroad as well as Warwick, Cambridge, Oxford Brookes and Edinburgh Universities. Lynne edits several maths and education journals.

**Jennifer Piggott** is a lecturer in mathematics enrichment and communication technology at Cambridge University. She is Director of the NRICH mathematics project and is part of the eastern region coordination team for the NCETM (National Centre for Excellence in the Teaching of Mathematics). Jennifer is an experienced mathematics and ICT teacher.

## Music

**Jonathan Savage** is a senior lecturer in music education at the Institute of Education, Manchester Metropolitan University. Until 2001 he was head of music at Debenham High School, an 11–16 comprehensive school in Suffolk. He is a co-author of a new resource introducing computer game sound design to the Key Stage 3 curriculum (www.sound2game.net) and managing director of UCan.tv (www.ucan.tv), a company specialising in the production of educational software and hardware. When not doing all of this, he is busy parenting four very musically talented children!

## Physical Education and Sport

**David Morley** has taught physical education in a number of secondary schools. He is currently senior lecturer in physical education at Leeds Metropolitan University and the director of the national DfES-funded 'Development in PE' project which is part of the Gifted and Talented strand of the PE, School Sport and Club Links (PESSCL) project. He is also a member of the team responsible for developing resources for national Multi-skill Clubs and is the founder and director of the Carnegie Regional Multi-skill Camp held at Leeds Met Carnegie.

**Richard Bailey** is professor of pedagogy at Roehampton University, having previously worked at Reading and Leeds Metropolitan University, and at Canterbury Christ Church University where he was director of the Centre for Physical Education Research. He is a well-known author and speaker on physical education, sport and education.

# Online content on the Routledge website

The online material accompanying this book may be used by the purchasing individual/organisation only. The files may be amended to suit particular situations, or individual learning needs, and printed out for use by the purchaser. The material can be accessed at www.routledge.com/education/fultonresources.asp.

www.routledge.com/education

# Introduction

## Who should use this book?

This book is for all teachers of religious education working with Key Stage 3 and Key Stage 4 pupils. It will be relevant to teachers working within the full spectrum of schools, from highly selective establishments to comprehensive and secondary modern schools as well as some special schools. Its overall objective is to provide a practical resource that heads of department, gifted and talented coordinators, leading teachers for gifted and talented education and classroom teachers can use to develop a coherent approach to provision for their most able pupils.

## Why is it needed?

School populations differ greatly and pupils considered very able in one setting might not stand out in another. Nevertheless, whatever the general level of ability within a school, there has been a tendency to plan and provide for the middle range, to modify for those who are struggling and to leave the most able to 'get on with it'. This has meant that the most able have:

- not been sufficiently challenged and stimulated

- underachieved

- been unaware of what they might be capable of achieving

- been unaware of what they need to do to achieve at the highest level

- not had high enough ambitions and aspirations

- sometimes become disaffected.

## How will this book help teachers?

This book and its accompanying website will, through its combination of practical ideas, materials for photocopying or downloading, and case studies:

- help teachers of RE to focus on the top 5–10% of the ability range in their particular school and to find ways of providing for these pupils, both within and beyond the classroom

- equip them with strategies and ideas to support exceptionally able pupils, i.e. those in the top 5% nationally.

## Terminology

The terms 'more able', 'most able' and 'exceptionally able' will generally be used in this series.

When 'gifted' and 'talented' are used, the definitions provided by the Department for Education and Skills (DfES) in its Excellence in Cities programme will apply. That is:

- **gifted** pupils are the most academically able in a school. This ability might be general or specific to a particular subject area, such as mathematics.

- **talented** pupils are those with high ability or potential in art, music, performing arts or sport.

The two groups together should form 5–10% of any school population.

There are, of course, some pupils who are both gifted and talented. Examples that come to mind are the budding physicist who plays the violin to a high standard in his spare time, or the pupil with high general academic ability who plays for the area football team.

This book is part of a series dealing with providing challenge for the most able secondary age pupils in a range of subjects. It is likely that some of the books in the series might also contain ideas that would be relevant to teachers of RE.

CHAPTER 1

# Our more able pupils – the national scene

- Making good provision for the most able – what's in it for schools?
- National initiatives since 1997
- *Every Child Matters* and the Children Act 2004
- *Higher Standards, Better Schools for All* – Education White Paper, October 2005
- Self-evaluation and inspection
- Resources for teachers and parents of more able pupils

Today's gifted pupils are tomorrow's social, intellectual, economic and cultural leaders and their development cannot be left to chance.

(Deborah Eyre, director of the National Academy for Gifted and Talented Youth, 2004)

The debate about whether to make special provision for the most able pupils in secondary schools ran its course during the last decade of the twentieth century. Explicit provision to meet their learning needs is now considered neither elitist nor a luxury. From an inclusion angle these pupils must have the same chances as others to develop their potential to the full. We know from international research that focusing on the needs of the most able changes teachers' perceptions of the needs of all their pupils, and there follows a consequential rise in standards. But for teachers who are not convinced by the inclusion or school improvement arguments, there is a much more pragmatic reason for meeting the needs of able pupils. Of course, it is preferable that colleagues share a common willingness to address the needs of the most able, but if they don't, it can at least be pointed out that, quite simply, it is something that all teachers are now required to do, not an optional extra.

All schools should seek to create an atmosphere in which to excel is not only acceptable but desirable.

(*Excellence in Schools* – DfEE 1997)

High achievement is determined by 'the school's commitment to inclusion and the steps it takes to ensure that every pupil does as well as possible'.

(*Handbook for Inspecting Secondary Schools* – Ofsted 2003)

A few years ago, efforts to raise standards in schools concentrated on getting as many pupils as possible over the Level 5 hurdle at the end of Key Stage 3 and over the 5 A*–C grades hurdle at GCSE. Resources were pumped into borderline pupils and the most able were not, on the whole, considered a cause for concern. The situation has changed dramatically in the last nine years with schools being expected to set targets for A*s and As and to show added value by helping pupils entering the school with high SATs scores to achieve Levels 7 and beyond, if supporting data suggests that that is what is achievable. Early recognition of high potential and the setting of curricular targets are at last addressing the lack of progress demonstrated by many able pupils in Year 7 and more attention is being paid to creating a climate in which learning can flourish. But there is a push for even more support for the most able through the promotion of personalised learning.

> The goal is that five years from now: gifted and talented students progress in line with their ability rather than their age; schools inform parents about tailored provision in an annual school profile; curricula include a gifted and talented dimension and at 14–19 there is more stretch and differentiation at the top end, so no matter what your talent it will be engaged; and the effect of poverty on achievement is reduced, because support for high-ability students from poorer backgrounds enables them to thrive.
>
> (Speech at National Academy for Gifted and Talented Youth – David Miliband, Minister for State for School Standards, May 2004)

It is hoped that this book, with the others in this series, will help to accelerate these changes.

## Making good provision for the most able – what's in it for schools?

Schools and/or subject departments often approach provision for the most able pupils with some reluctance because they imagine a lot of extra work for very little reward. In fact, the rewards of providing for these pupils are substantial.

- It can be very stimulating to the subject specialist to explore ways of developing approaches with enthusiastic and able students.

> Taking a serious look at what I should expect from the most able and then at how I should teach them has given my teaching a new lease of life. I feel so sorry for youngsters who were taught by me ten years ago. They must have been bored beyond belief. But then, to be quite honest, so was I.
>
> (Science teacher)

- Offering opportunities to tackle work in a more challenging manner often interests pupils whose abilities have gone unnoticed because they have not been motivated by a bland educational diet.

> Some of the others were invited to an after-school maths club. When I heard what they were doing, it sounded so interesting that I asked the maths teacher if I could go too. She was a bit doubtful at first because I have messed about a lot but she agreed to take me on trial. I'm one of her star pupils now and she reckons I'll easily get an A*. I still find some of the lessons really slow and boring but I don't mess around – well, not too much.
>
> (Year 10 boy)

- When pupils are engaged by the work they are doing motivation, attainment and discipline improve.

> You don't need to be gifted to work out that the work we do is much more interesting and exciting. It's made others want to be like us.
> (Comment of a student involved in an extension programme for the most able)

- Schools identified as very good by Ofsted generally have good provision for their most able students.

> If you are willing to deal effectively with the needs of able pupils you will raise the achievement of all pupils.
> (Mike Tomlinson, former director of Ofsted)

- The same is true of individual departments in secondary schools. All those considered to be very good have spent time developing a sound working approach that meets the needs of their most able pupils.

> The department creates a positive atmosphere by its organisation, display and the way that students are valued. Learning is generally very good and often excellent throughout the school. The teachers' high expectations permeate the atmosphere and are a significant factor in raising achievement. These expectations are reflected in the curriculum which has depth and students are able and expected to experience difficult problems in all year groups.
> (Mathematics Department, Hamstead Hall School, Birmingham; Ofsted 2003)

## National initiatives since 1997

In 1997, the new government demonstrated its commitment to gifted and talented education by setting up a Gifted and Talented Advisory Group (GTAG). Since then there has been a wide range of government and government-funded initiatives that have, either directly or indirectly, impacted on our most able pupils and their teachers. Details of some can be found below. Others that relate to RE will be found later in this book.

## Excellence in Cities

In an attempt to deal with the chronic underachievement of able pupils in inner city areas, Excellence in Cities (EiC) was launched in 1999. This was a very ambitious, well-funded programme with many different strands. In the first place it concentrated on secondary age pupils but work was extended into the primary sector in many areas. Provision for gifted and talented students was one of the strands.

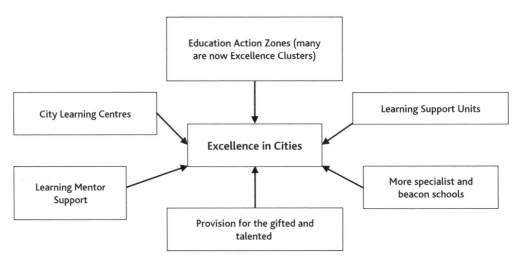

Strands in the Excellence in Cities Initiative

EiC schools were expected to:

- develop a whole-school policy for their most able pupils

- appoint a gifted and talented coordinator with sufficient time to fulfil the role

- send the coordinator on a national training programme run by Oxford Brookes University

- identify 5–10% of pupils in each year group as their gifted and talented cohort, the gifted being the academically able and the talented being those with latent or obvious ability in PE, sport, music, art or the performing arts

- provide an appropriate programme of work both within the school day and beyond

- set 'aspirational' targets both for the gifted and talented cohort as a whole and for individual pupils

- work with other schools in a 'cluster' to provide further support for these pupils

- work with other agencies, such as Aimhigher, universities, businesses and private sector schools, to enhance provision and opportunities for these pupils.

Funding changes have meant that schools no longer receive dedicated EiC money through local authorities but the lessons learned from EiC have been influential in developing a national approach to gifted and talented education. All schools are now expected to adopt similar strategies to ensure that the needs of their most able students are met.

## Excellence Clusters

Although EiC was set up initially in the main urban conurbations, other hot spots of underachievement and poverty were also identified and Excellence Clusters were established. For example, Ellesmere Port, Crewe and Barrow-in-Furness are pockets of deprivation, with major social problems and significant underachievement, in otherwise affluent areas. Excellence Clusters have been established in these three places and measures are being taken to improve provision for the most able pupils. The approach is similar to that used in Excellence in Cities areas.

## Aimhigher

Aimhigher is another initiative of the Department for Education and Skills (DfES) working in partnership with the Higher Education Funding Council for England (HEFCE). Its remit is to widen participation in UK higher education, particularly among students from groups that do not have a tradition of going to university, such as some ethnic minorities, the disabled and those from poorer homes. Both higher education institutions and secondary schools have Aimhigher coordinators who work together to identify pupils who would benefit from additional support and to plan a programme of activities. Opportunities are likely to include:

- mentoring, including e-mentoring

- residential summer schools

- visits to different campuses and university departments

- masterclasses

- online information for students and parents

- advice on the wide range of financial and other support available to disadvantaged students.

One national Aimhigher project, Higher Education Gateway, is specifically targeted on gifted and talented students from disadvantaged groups. More information can be found at www.aimhigher.ac.uk.

## National Academy for Gifted and Talented Youth (NAGTY)

Government initiatives have not been confined to the most able pupils in deprived areas. In 2002, the National Academy for Gifted and Talented Youth was established at Warwick University. Its brief was to offer support to the most able 5% of the school population and their teachers and parents. It did this in a number of ways:

| National Academy for Gifted and Talented Youth | | |
|---|---|---|
| **Student Academy** | **Professional Academy** | **Expertise Centre** |
| • Summer schools including link-ups with CTY in USA.<br>• Outreach courses in a wide range of subjects at universities and other venues across the country.<br>• Online activities – currently maths, classics, ethics, philosophy. | • Continuing professional development for teachers.<br>• A PGCE+ programme for trainee teachers.<br>• Ambassador School Programme to disseminate good practice amongst schools. | • Leading research in gifted and talented education. |

NAGTY worked closely with the DfES with the latter setting policy and NAGTY increasingly taking the lead in the practical application of this policy – a policy known as the English Model, which, as explained on NAGTY's website, is 'rooted in day-to-day classroom provision and enhanced by additional, more advanced opportunities offered both within school and outside of it'. NAGTY ceased operation in August 2007 and was replaced by the Young, Gifted & Talented Programme (see below).

## The Young, Gifted & Talented Programme (YG&T)

In December 2006, the UK government announced the creation of a new programme in England, the National Programme for Gifted and Talented Education (NPGATE), to be managed by CfBT Education Trust and now known as the Young, Gifted & Talented Programme (YG&T). Among the changes proposed are:

- a much greater emphasis on school and local level provision.

- the setting-up of Excellence Hubs – HEI-led partnerships to provide non-residential summer schools and a diverse range of outreach provision, including summer activities, weekend events and online and blended learning models. There will be free places for the disadvantaged.

- the appointment of gifted and talented leading teachers – one for each secondary school and each cluster of primary schools.

- a national training programme for gifted and talented leading teachers organised by the national primary and secondary strategies.

Further information about YG&T can be found at www.dfes.gov.uk/ygt and www.cfbt.com.

## Gifted and talented summer schools

Education authorities are encouraged to work in partnership with schools to run a number of summer schools (dependent on the size of the authority) for the most able pupils in Years 6–11. It is expected that there will be a particular emphasis on transition and that around 50 hours of tuition will be offered. Some schools and authorities run summer schools for up to ten days whilst others cover a shorter period and have follow-up sessions or even residential weekends later in the school year. Obviously the main aim is to challenge and stimulate these pupils but the DfES also hopes that:

- they will encourage teachers and advisers to adopt innovative teaching approaches

- teachers will continue to monitor these pupils over time

- where Year 6 pupils are involved, it will make secondary teachers aware of what they can achieve and raise their expectations of Year 7 pupils.

More can be found out about these summer schools at www.standards.dfes. gov.uk/giftedandtalented. Funding for them has now been incorporated into the school development grant.

## Regional partnerships

When Excellence in Cities (EiC) was first introduced, gifted and talented strand coordinators from different EiC partnerships began to meet up with others in their regions to explore ways of working together so that the task would be more manageable and resources could be pooled. One of the most successful examples of cooperation was the Trans-Pennine Group that started up in the northwest. It began to organise training on a regional basis as well as masterclasses and other activities for some gifted and talented pupils. The success of this and other groups led to the setting-up of nine regional partnerships with initial support from NAGTY and finance from DfES. Each partnership had a steering group composed of representatives from local authorities, higher education institutions, regional organisations concerned with gifted and talented children and NAGTY. Each regional partnership organised professional training; sought to support schools and areas in greatest need; tried to ensure that all 11- to 19-year-olds who fell into the top 5% of the ability range were registered with NAGTY; provided opportunities for practitioner research and arranged challenging activities for pupils. Under the YG&T Programme, nine Excellence Hubs have been created to continue and expand the work of the regional partnerships.

## *Every Child Matters: Change for Children* and the Children Act 2004

The likelihood of all children reaching their potential has always been hampered by the fragmented nature of agencies concerned with provision for them. Vital information held by an agency about a child's needs has often been kept back from other agencies, including schools. This has had a particularly negative impact on the disadvantaged, for example, looked-after children. In 2004, 57% of looked-after children left school without even one GCSE or GNVQ and only 6% achieved five or more good GCSEs (see national statistics at www.dfes.gov.uk/rsgateway/). This represents a huge waste of national talent as well as many personal tragedies.

The Children Act 2004 sought to overcome these problems by, amongst other things, requiring:

- local authorities to make arrangements to promote cooperation between agencies to ensure the well-being of all children

- all children's services to bear these five outcomes in mind when planning provision. Children should:

  - be healthy

  - stay safe

  - enjoy and achieve

  - make a positive contribution

  - achieve economic well-being.

There are major implications for schools in seeking to achieve these outcomes for their most able pupils, especially where there is deprivation and/or low aspiration:

- local authorities to appoint a director of children's services to coordinate education and social services

- each local authority to take on the role of corporate parent to promote the educational achievement of looked-after children. This should help to ensure that greater consideration is given to their education when changes in foster placements are being considered

- the setting-up of an integrated inspection regime to look at the totality of provision for children.

More information can be found at www.everychildmatters.gov.uk.

## *Higher Standards, Better Schools for All* (Education White Paper, October 2005)

Although the thrust of this Education White Paper is to improve educational opportunities for all, there is no doubt that some proposals will particularly benefit the most able, especially those that are disadvantaged in some way.

- Pupils receiving free school meals will be able to get **free public transport** to any one of three secondary schools closest to their homes between two and six miles away. At present, such children have very little choice in secondary schooling because their parents cannot afford the fares. This measure will allow them access to schools that might be better able to cater for their particular strengths and needs.

- **The National Register of Gifted and Talented Learners** will record the top 5% of the nation's children, as identified by a wide range of measures, so that they can be tracked and supported throughout their school careers. At first, the focus will be on 11- to 19-year-olds but later identification will start at the age of 4. As a first step, in 2006 all secondary schools were asked to identify gifted and talented students in the school census. In reality, some authorities had already begun this monitoring process but making it a national priority will bring other schools and authorities up to speed.

- In line with new school managerial structures, **'leading teachers' of the gifted and talented** will take the place of gifted and talented coordinators. Training (optionally accredited) will be organised through the national strategies. Leading teachers will work closely with School Improvement Partners and local authority coordinators to implement G& T improvement plans, and undertake much of the work previously undertaken by school coordinators.

- **Additional training** in providing for gifted and talented pupils will be available to all schools.

- **A national programme of non-residential summer schools** will be organised to run alongside gifted and talented summer schools already provided by local authorities and individual schools.

- Secondary schools will be encouraged to make greater use of **grouping by ability** in order to meet the needs of the most able and to use **curriculum flexibility** to allow pupils to take Key Stage 3 tests and GCSE courses early and to mix academic and vocational courses.

- **At advanced level, a new extended project** will allow the most able students to demonstrate high scholastic ability.

- **Extended schools** (see later section).

- **More personalised learning** (see later section).

More information on *Higher Standards, Better Schools for All* can be found at www.dfes.gov.uk/publications/schoolswhitepaper.

## Extended schools

In many parts of the country, extended schools are already operating, but it is intended that schools will become much more central in providing a wide range of services to children, parents and the community. The government intends to spend £680 million by 2008 to facilitate these developments. Ideally these services should include:

- all-year childcare from 8.00am to 6.00pm

- referral to a wide range of support services, such as speech therapy, mental health and behaviour support

- exciting activities, including study support and extension/enrichment activities that will motivate the most able

- parenting support, which might include classes on healthy eating, helping children with homework, dealing with challenging behaviour etc

- community use of school facilities, especially ICT.

Again, this is an initiative that will benefit all children, especially those whose carers work. However, there are particular benefits for those children whose school performance suffers because they have nowhere to study at home and for those with talents that parents cannot nurture because of limited means.

More information on Extended Schools can be found at www.teachernet.gov.uk/settingup and www.tda.gov.uk/remodelling/extendedschools.aspx.

## Personalised learning

As mentioned earlier in this chapter, a key component of current education reforms is the emphasis on personalised learning – maximising potential by tailoring education to individual needs, strengths and interests. The key features of personalised learning are:

- **Assessment for Learning** – Information from data and the tasks and assessments pupils undertake must be used to feed back suggestions about how work could be improved and what learning they need to do next. But the feedback should be a two-way process with pupils also providing information to teachers about factors impeding their learning and approaches that would enhance it. This feedback should inform future lesson planning. For the most able pupils, effective assessment for learning should mean that they move forward with their learning at an appropriate pace and depth, rather than marking time while others catch up.

- **Effective Teaching and Learning Strategies** – It is still the case that many teachers teach only in the way that was most successful for them as learners. There is ample evidence that our most able pupils do not form an homogeneous group and that, in order to bring out their many and varied gifts and talents, we need to adopt a wide range of teaching strategies, making full use of the opportunities provided by ICT. At the same time pupils need to become aware of the learning strategies that are most successful for them, whilst also exploring a broader range of learning approaches.

- **Curriculum Entitlement and Choice** – There are many examples of highly gifted adults whose abilities were masked at school because the curriculum did not appear to be relevant to them. Schools need to take the opportunities afforded by new flexibility in the curriculum, by the specialised diplomas of study being introduced for 14- to 19-year-olds and by partnership with other schools, colleges and businesses to engage their pupils. There are several schools now where more able pupils cover Key Stage 3 in two years. The year that is freed up by this approach can be used in a variety of ways, such as starting GCSE courses early, following an enrichment programme or taking up additional science and language courses. The possibilities are endless if there is desire for change.

- **School Organisation** – Effective personalisation demands a more flexible approach to school organisation. This flexibility might show itself in the way teaching and support staff are deployed, by the way pupils are grouped, by the structure of the school day and by the way in which ICT is used to enable learning to take place beyond the classroom. At least one school is abandoning grouping by age in favour of grouping by ability in the hope that this will provide the necessary challenge for the most able. It remains to be seen how successful this approach is but experimentation and risk-taking is essential if we are to make schooling relevant and exciting for our most able pupils.

- **Partnerships Beyond Schools** – Schools cannot provide adequately for their most able pupils without making full use of the opportunities and expertise offered by other groups within the community, including parents together with family support groups, social and health services, sports clubs and other recreational and business organisations.

The websites www.standards.dfes.gov.uk/personalisedlearning and www.teacher net.gov.uk/publications/ will provide more information on personalised learning, whilst new curriculum opportunities to be offered to 14- to 19-year-olds are described in www.dfes.gov.uk/14-19.

## Self-evaluation and inspection

The most able must have as many opportunities for development as other pupils. Poor, unchallenging teaching or an ideology that confuses equality of opportunity with levelling down should not hinder their progress. They should have a fair share of a school's resources both in terms of learning materials and in human resources. The environment for learning should be one in which it is safe to be clever and to excel. These are points that schools should consider when preparing their self-evaluation and school development plans.

There have been dramatic changes in the relationships between schools and local authorities and in the schools' inspection regime since the Children Act 2004. Local authorities are now regarded as commissioners for services for children. One of their tasks is to facilitate the appointment of SIPs, School Improvement Partners, who act as the main conduit between schools and LAs and take part in an 'annual conversation' with their schools when the school's self-evaluation and progress towards targets is discussed.

Self-evaluation is also the cornerstone of the new shorter, more frequent Ofsted inspections, using a SEF (self-evaluation form) as a central point of reference together with the five outcomes for children of *Every Child Matters*. An invaluable tool for schools recognising that they need to do more for their gifted and talented pupils, or simply wanting to assess their current provision, is the institutional quality standards for gifted and talented education (IQS).

## Institutional quality standards for gifted and talented education (IQS)

These standards, developed by a partnership of the DfES, NAGTY and other interested groups, are an essential self-evaluation tool for any school focusing on its gifted and talented provision. Under each of five headings, schools look carefully at the level indicators and decide which of the three levels they have achieved:

● **Entry level** – a school making its first steps towards developing a whole-school policy might find that much of its provision falls into this category. Ofsted would rate such provision satisfactory.

● **Developing level** – where there is some effective practice but there is room for development and improvement. This aligns with a good from Ofsted.

● **Exemplary level** – where good practice is exceptional and sustained. Ofsted would rate this excellent.

The five headings show clear links to the personalisation agenda: effective teaching and learning strategies; enabling curriculum entitlement and choice; assessment for learning; school organisation; and strong partnerships beyond school.

Having identified the levels at which they are performing, schools are then able to draw up development plans. A copy of these standards is included in the appendices and more information about them can be found at www2.teachernet.gov.uk/qualitystandards.

## Resources for teachers and parents of more able pupils

There is currently an abundance of resources and support agencies for teachers, parents and gifted and talented young people themselves. A few of general interest are included below. Other religious education examples will be found in later chapters of this book.

### World Class Tests

These have been introduced by QCA to allow schools to judge the performance of their most able pupils against national and international standards. Currently tests are available for 9- and 13-year-olds in mathematics and problem solving. Some schools have found that the problem solving tests are effective at identifying able underachievers in maths and science. The website contains sample questions so that teachers, parents and pupils themselves can assess the tests' suitability for particular pupils or groups of pupils, and the tests themselves are also available online. For more information go to www.worldclassarena. org.uk.

### National Curriculum Online

This website, administered by QCA, provides general guidance on all aspects of the national curriculum but also has a substantial section on general and subject-specific issues relating to gifted and talented education, including identification strategies, case studies, management and units of work. Details of the National Curriculum Online can be found at www.nc.uk.net/gt.

### G&TWise

G&TWise links to recommended resources for gifted and talented pupils, checked by professionally qualified subject editors, in all subjects and at all key stages and provides up-to-date information for teachers on gifted and talented education. Details can be found at www2.teachernet.gov.uk.

### NACE – the National Association for Able Children in Education

NACE is an independent organisation that offers support for teachers and other professionals trying to develop provision for gifted and talented pupils. It gives advice and guidance to teachers and others, runs courses and conferences, provides consultants and keynote speakers.

It has also produced the NACE Challenge Award Framework, which it recommends could be used alongside IQS, as it exemplifies evidence and action planning. While IQS indicates what needs to be improved, the Challenge Award Framework suggests how to effect change. More information can be found at www.nace.co.uk.

## National Association for Gifted Children (NAGC)

NAGC is a charity providing support for gifted and talented children and young people and their parents and teachers. It has a regional structure and in some parts of the country there are branch activities for children and parents. NAGC provides: counselling for both young people and their parents; INSET and courses for teachers; publications; activities for 3- to 10-year-olds; and a dedicated area on their website for 11- to 19-year-olds (to which they have exclusive access), called Youth Agency. For further information go to www.nagcbritain.org.uk.

## Children of High Intelligence (CHI)

CHI acts on behalf of children whose intelligence puts them above the 98th percentile. It often acts in a support capacity when parents are negotiating appropriate provision with schools and local authorities. For further details visit www.chi-charity.org.uk.

## Summary

- Schools must provide suitable challenge and support for their most able pupils.
- Appropriate provision can enhance motivation and improve behaviour.
- Recent legislation to support disadvantaged children should mean that fewer potentially gifted and talented children fall through the net.
- Effective self-evaluation of school provision for gifted and talented pupils and challenging targets are the keys to progress.
- There are many agencies that can help teachers with this work.

CHAPTER 2

# Departmental policy and approach

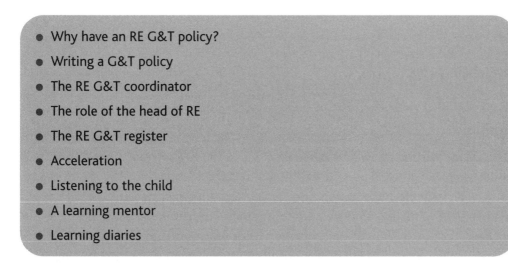

- Why have an RE G&T policy?
- Writing a G&T policy
- The RE G&T coordinator
- The role of the head of RE
- The RE G&T register
- Acceleration
- Listening to the child
- A learning mentor
- Learning diaries

## Why have an RE G&T policy?

Teachers of RE, indeed all teachers, are confronted with a relentless list of things which have to be undertaken: prepare lessons, mark books, plan homework, organise resources, attend meetings, sort out the classroom display, teach – the list is formidable. To add to that list yet another item, write a G&T policy which describes how the department meets the needs of young people gifted in RE, will not come as welcome news. Given what seems like yet another task, many teachers who have responsibility for RE in their school will ask the question, 'Does an RE department have to have a G&T policy?'

To be brutally honest, the strict answer to that question is 'no'. It is possible that an RE department could be making excellent provision for its gifted students and yet how it does so may not be written down. Clearly, it is delivery that is important, not paperwork. In a department where there is only one key person teaching RE, how they go about meeting the needs of more able pupils might not be committed to paper. Similarly, in a small department with only one specialist teacher and perhaps one other person, an effective G&T policy might be little more than an appendix or an additional paragraph or two to the department's policy. However, this is the exception rather than the rule. Most departments, large or small, that have enjoyed some success with their more able students have a well-considered and clear G&T policy.

An RE department's policy for teaching more able pupils should spell out for parents, inspectors, supply staff, other members of the department or anyone else interested how the subject will support and challenge the more able pupils. However, above all a G&T policy should clarify the thinking and focus the efforts of all the people who teach RE in a school. Through the process of producing a policy there should emerge a clear understanding of how young people who have a flair for RE will be extended and challenged. Of course, an RE policy must reflect what really happens in the department. It must not be a piece of fictitious window dressing. A policy must also have the broad agreement and support of the staff involved in teaching RE. There is also little point in writing a document which merely sits in a filing cabinet unread. It must be a working document, which is known, understood and acted upon.

## Writing a G&T policy

### An audit

Usually the writing of an RE G&T policy will start with an audit. An audit is best undertaken by all teachers and teaching assistants involved in RE. The idea is to gather all available information and review current practice with regard to how the needs of more able children are being met within the department. Everyone in the department should feel that they have an input into the development of the policy. Because of this it is important to ensure that everyone is aware that a policy statement is being prepared and that the ideas and views of everyone involved in implementing the policy are being sought.

The auditing process should be seen as an opportunity for professional development and as an exercise in sharing good practice. The local authority's RE adviser, or the diocesan adviser, might be invited to attend a department meeting. At such a meeting they might be asked to provide an introduction to teaching RE to more able children. By doing so misconceptions, for example, fears about elitism, might be dealt with leaving the way open for a productive and informed discussion.

An audit might also encourage thoughtful discussion about what the department needs to give priority to. Perhaps, for example, early on in the process there emerges a broad agreement that students' verbal contributions in the classroom are often limited to single clause or even single word responses. Or perhaps the department has very little knowledge of what its primary feeder schools are providing for pupils gifted in RE. Because of this some children may be repeating work in Year 7 that they are already familiar with and are quickly becoming disenchanted with a subject they previously loved. If such issues emerge it may be appropriate to take positive steps quickly to try and remedy the situation and not wait until a formal policy statement has been written.

## The main headings of an RE G&T policy

Every RE department's more able child or G&T policy is different. However, a helpful policy is likely to make use of the following headings.

### General statement

- What are the school's main aims?
- What does the school's G&T policy say?
- What does the agreed syllabus, diocesan syllabus, SACRE or local authority say about RE and the more able child?

### Definition of a 'gifted' or more able child in RE

- What does being 'gifted' in RE mean?
- What criteria will be used to identify children 'gifted' in RE?

### General provision

- Will someone have special responsibility for G&T pupils within the department?
- What will be the role of the RE G&T coordinator?
- Will a register of pupils 'gifted' in RE be kept?
- How and when is information about the RE 'gifted' register shared?

### Classroom provision for more able pupils

- What teaching strategies will be used to meet the needs of more able pupils?
- How will the scheme of work meet the needs of more able pupils?
- How are teaching groups to be organised?
- How will differentiation be undertaken?
- What are the arrangements for acceleration, enrichment and extension?

### Out-of-school-hours provision

- How will out-of-school-hours provision, e.g. clubs, summer schools, residentials, meet the needs of more able pupils?
- How will homework and extended personal assignments meet the needs of more able pupils?
- What use will be made of outside agencies and other providers?

### Continuing professional development

- What training or qualifications do members of the department have?
- What are the arrangements for CPD?

## Monitoring and reviewing the policy

- How will the RE G&T policy be monitored?
- How will the RE G&T policy be reviewed?

## The RE G&T coordinator

Crucial to effective provision for more able pupils in RE is the role of the RE G&T coordinator. An RE G&T coordinator is a member of the RE teaching staff who oversees and takes special responsibility for the progress of those students who are particularly gifted in the subject. In many schools where there is only a small team of RE teachers this might be a role for the second senior member of the RE team. In some cases, perhaps the role will be one which the head of the department or subject leader will wish to undertake. Ideally the post should carry with it some remuneration. It should not be half-heartedly fobbed off onto a member of the team who has little time or commitment to G&T education, or has little weight with other members of the department.

## The role of the RE G&T coordinator

The main role of the RE G&T coordinator can be described under six broad headings. These are:

- pupil achievement
- assessment and evaluation
- staff development
- parents and the wider community
- strategic leadership
- managing resources.

### Pupil achievement

This part of the job involves developing effective teaching strategies for pupils gifted in RE. The RE G&T coordinator will not only be concerned to develop appropriate teaching and learning activities in their own classroom. They will also work with colleagues in the RE department in order to discuss and share ideas, evaluate what works and disseminate good practice with other colleagues. As well as seeking to support the learning of gifted students in the RE classroom, the RE G&T coordinator will also be working with colleagues to develop appropriately challenging out-of-school activities, for example, differentiated homework, an RE and Philosophy Club, visits to museums, exhibitions or conferences.

## Assessment and evaluation

This involves advising members of the RE team on effective strategies for identifying young people gifted in RE. The RE G&T coordinator, drawing upon the views and suggestions of other members of the RE team, would be the main person responsible for creating a register of pupils gifted in RE. They would monitor and regularly check that register to ensure that there is no inappropriate social, religious, racial or gender bias. They would also regularly update the information on the register, using information gained from colleagues and other sources, and keep members of the RE team informed about any new relevant information. For example, they may feed back information about the progress and achievement of individual pupils on the register. The G&T coordinator, for example, may report that Nassem in Year 9 has completed his special assignment on the relationship between salah and zakat in Islamic thinking and that this will be posted on the school's RE website. He has also won a place on a summer school for which the school is paying half of the cost out of the gifted and talented summer school budget.

Or perhaps, in some cases, a student on the register may be underachieving due to particular circumstances which need to be shared with colleagues and discussed in order to find ways of best supporting the child. Assessment and evaluation also involves interpreting relevant national, local, school and pupil data, and also any transition information, in order to evaluate how well the RE department is doing. This information will often form a substantial part of a department's self-evaluation process and so will be fed back to the subject leader, and in turn to the headteacher, the governing body and to the LA. Feedback to the LA might be through the local authority's RE adviser or to the local authority's SACRE. SACREs, or the Standing Advisory Councils for Religious Education, are local LA advisory councils made up of representatives of teachers, faith communities and councillors. Every local authority's SACRE has a legal obligation to monitor and evaluate the local standards and quality of RE. For this reason all SACREs are interested in how effectively young people in the local area, including the more able, are taught RE.

## Staff development

The RE G&T coordinator needs to be able to work with the other members of staff who teach RE providing them with feedback, support and advice in order to develop their effectiveness in meeting the needs of pupils gifted in RE. They may liaise with the CPD coordinator, and network with other teachers and other schools in order to find sources of effective professional development which they and other members of the RE team can work with and learn from.

## Parents and the wider community

This part of the job involves developing a good relationship with parents and carers of pupils gifted in RE. This may involve helping parents and carers to understand how they can support their child's learning and development. So, for example, a parent may be encouraged to take a much more active role in supporting the progress of their child by:

- showing a lot more interest, e.g. asking, 'What did you do in RE today?' or by encouraging their child to take a more active interest by saying things like 'Have you asked a good question in RE recently?'

- extending at home through discussion the child's learning and understanding, for example, a parent might stimulate discussion at home with a question like 'So, if Buddhists meditate how is that different from worship?' or 'If Jesus is the Son of God, what does that mean? Aren't we all sons or daughters of God?'

- helping the child to access sources of information and ideas, e.g. books, websites, TV and radio programmes, galleries, museums, places of religious significance.

- participating in school events arranged by the RE department, e.g. visits to places of worship, special exhibitions, RE conferences for students.

- supporting their child's interest in a Saturday morning outreach course, e.g. taking their child to a botanical garden for a course on 'Does life have a meaning?'

Gifted children can be extremely demanding. They may have a voracious appetite for learning and a passion for ideas. To help such children to develop their potential it may well be desirable for both the school and the home to combine their efforts. Also the RE G&T coordinator should attempt to develop partnerships with other schools in order that they may learn from each other and collaborate on joint projects; for example, three schools may pool their resources and set up an inter-school RE conference involving keynote speakers and workshop leaders. The coordinator should also be aware of outside agencies and encourage and support pupils they identify as being suitable members.

### Strategic leadership

Although the head of the department is primarily responsible for strategic leadership they may well look to the RE G&T coordinator to help determine what the department might do in order to improve still further its provision for very able pupils. For example, developing changes in the scheme of work by introducing a more values- and ideas-based RE may originally arise from ideas proposed by the G&T coordinator.

### Managing resources

The RE G&T coordinator should identify and make available both material and human resources which can improve the quality of provision for very able children. They would be responsible for expenditure on resources which support the teaching of very able children gifted in RE and ensure value for money.

Substantial though the role of the RE G&T coordinator is, the progress of more able pupils is a job for everyone in the RE team, not just one person. Effective RE provision for more able pupils cannot be achieved by bolt-on additions like Saturday morning masterclasses, RE clubs or special trips. These are all well and good but the main forum for supporting more able pupils in RE is in the classroom. Every RE teacher in the department must play their part to ensure that they are aware of particularly able children in their classrooms and that in the course of the lessons they teach these pupils are stretched and challenged. The involvement of the head of RE can be crucial in ensuring that this happens.

# The role of the head of RE

## Set an ethos and climate

The head of RE is the primary person setting the ethos and climate within the department who drives the commitment to effective teaching of able children. By frequently talking to colleagues about their lessons, how able children are making progress, by ensuring that the issue of how to challenge able children is frequently on the agenda at department meetings, the head of the department can send out a clear message that challenging able pupils is to be taken seriously.

## Support lesson planning

The head of RE can directly help teachers to plan lessons which more effectively stretch able children by encouraging colleagues to discuss their lesson plans, by making suggestions and by giving advice on how an ordinary lesson can be turned into something which is much more stimulating and demanding.

## Peer coaching

A head of RE could set up within the department a peer coaching programme. Peer coaching involves teachers observing each other's lessons. This requires establishing a climate of trust and mutual respect. The emphasis is not on judging a fellow colleague's lesson. Instead it is about the insights and helpful observations fellow colleagues can share which enable them to better understand what does and what doesn't work in an RE classroom. It is not unlike the way in which two friends who play tennis may mutually coach and advise each other, spotting strengths and weaknesses in each other's play, which they would otherwise be unaware of. So also two colleagues may work together observing whenever possible each other's lessons and so refine and develop their skills as teachers of RE.

## Set targets

A head of RE could, either informally or more formally as part of a performance review, discuss with the RE G&T coordinator what progress the department has made in its provision for more able children. During this discussion the head of RE might guide, make suggestions, offer advice or, if necessary, steer the coordinator in a direction which results in more effective progress. The head of

RE might agree with the coordinator on particular targets. Targets should take the form of a clearly measurable outcome. Try to avoid targets which lend themselves to questionable interpretation. So for example, 'Our target next year is to stretch the more able pupils in our RE GCSE short course' might look like a clear target. However, whether or not it is achieved will come down to an uncertain judgement. A more clearly framed target like 'Our target next year is to achieve in our GCSE short course 17% A* or A' is not subject to the same doubts. Setting targets can give an individual a clear sense of direction and, if the target is achieved, a real sense of progress.

## Resources, funding and CPD

The head of RE should be the main person who puts the case to the headteacher or to the senior management to provide additional funding or support for the department's provision for more able children. This includes funding for CPD and any necessary release time in order to attend such training. Bids for external funding, for example Aimhigher funding or funding for a regional outreach programme, need to be actively supported by the head of the RE.

## Senior management, governors' review

The head of RE also has an important role in updating the headteacher, senior management and the governors on how the department's policy for supporting more able children is working. The head of RE and the RE G&T coordinator may decide to present such reviews jointly. What should not happen is the coordinator to be sent into a governors' or a senior management meeting where, depending on the success or otherwise of the G&T policy, they might face a grilling, while the head of RE is not present and takes no responsibility.

## Cross-curricular and whole-school strategies

The head of RE needs also to be involved in and supportive of any strategies for more able children which involve other departments. A national strategy like 'Leading in Learning' which involves a whole-school programme for teaching thinking skills is unlikely to have an effective impact on RE in the school if the head of RE is disengaged and leaves everything up to others in the department.

## Motivating and inspiring

Finally, another role of the head of RE is to motivate and inspire members of the RE teaching team as they perform their various duties, including the task of challenging more able children. Teaching can seem like a lonely world. Once a teacher of RE steps into a classroom and closes the door, whatever goes on in that lesson seems to be largely unobserved by others.

In the course of the lesson the teacher may, through a carefully constructed series of questions or perhaps through the use of a thoughtfully conceived analogy, help the children to grasp in a highly profound way the Christian belief in the incarnation. On such occasions children enjoy disclosure moments when genuine understanding takes place. So, for example, a very able child in the course of the lesson might say, 'So really, Miss, it wasn't just a man who suffered on the cross. That was God on the cross that was suffering!'

The head of RE needs to make it their business to know when successful lessons like this happen. When teachers do well in the classroom or when teachers are trying to raise the standards and try out new ideas – even when things don't go quite as well as they might have hoped – the head of RE should be acknowledging their efforts, praising their success and rewarding their dedication.

By talking to teachers and to children, by asking questions, by looking at exercise books and by visiting classrooms, an effective head of RE will actively seek out examples of good RE teaching. When they do they might take that teacher to one side and say something like 'I heard about your lesson on the incarnation the other day. I just wanted to say well done. It was an excellent piece of challenging teaching. Keep up the good work. I've spoken to the headteacher about your teaching and I know the head was really impressed as well.' Teachers of RE who work in small departments often have to be largely self-motivating individuals. But when others notice what they are doing and show their appreciation it can put a spring in their step. It can make the difference between a motivated workforce that is prepared to think creatively about their teaching, so that they develop lessons which drive children on and stimulate their curiosity, as opposed to lessons which are little more than safe, predictable, mundane or routine.

## The RE G&T register

Making effective use of the register of students gifted in RE must be an important part of a department's approach to supporting able children. To be useful the register must be more than a list of names, or a series of asterisks by names in a mark book. The register should be developed so that it provides the teacher of RE with information about the child's achievements, interests, strengths and weaknesses in the subject.

Every child is different and the potential field of study in RE is enormous. No child is likely to have a highly developed, comprehensive knowledge and insight into six or more principal religious traditions. Similarly, no child is likely to be able to provide a detailed and thoughtfully reasoned and balanced evaluation of all the different questions and issues which religious experience and human life may give rise to. Given that a child is unlikely to be equally gifted or interested in everything in the vast galaxy of matter called RE the register should reveal to the teacher something of the interest and turn of mind the child has shown. For example, the child may have a particular interest in Islam, has read several contemporary biographies about Muhammad, but is now interested in the development of Islamic law and the part the Sunnah of the Prophet plays in

Islamic decision making. Or another child may have a very extensive knowledge of Christian ritual and ceremony but is now interested in the theology of the liturgy and how it has developed over time.

Information of this kind can inform a much more personalised approach to the child's educational development. By directing the child towards sources of information, particular books and through the use of tailored activities and assignments, a very able child may be helped to make continued progress in RE. By supporting the child's development in areas in which they have shown interest or skills, the child's understanding is developed in depth. Breadth of knowledge is certainly one characteristic of a child gifted in RE. However, depth of insight and subtlety of understanding, which comes to an individual when they have pursued a particular aspect of RE in depth, is more often than not the major characteristic of a child gifted in RE.

## The register and inclusion

With any register of able students it is important to be alert to the dangers of insufficient representation of particular social, ethnic or gender groups. For example, the register may have relatively few boys and an inordinately high proportion of girls. Or maybe the register has a very small proportion of African-Caribbean students. Or perhaps the register has very few pupils who receive free school meals. Where such lack of representation exists in a register the teachers in the department need to be alert to the situation. Having been made aware of the situation, teachers need to consider if there is a bias in their selection of students for the register which they need to acknowledge and take steps to eliminate. A register of students gifted in RE is not a register of students who are the 'teachers' favoured' because they are merely compliant, neat, hardworking, helpful or responsive in the classroom. A register should contain students who, because of our own unaware assumptions, we may overlook or have a tendency not to recognise.

## Acceleration

As part of its general approach to ensuring effective challenge for very able pupils in RE, a department might need to consider its policy on acceleration. Acceleration involves taking a very able pupil out of their normal teaching group and placing them in an older class. So, for example, a bright child may be taken out of their Year 7 RE class and taught instead with a Year 8, Year 9 or an even older class.

The reasoning behind such a decision is clear enough. Such is the child's mental maturity that the level of challenge they would receive in their Year 7 class is not sufficient to meet their needs effectively. The problem cannot be effectively resolved by keeping the child with their own age group and providing differentiated work. Given the level of discussion and ideas going on in the classroom, keeping the child in their Year 7 class is simply holding the child back.

Another example of acceleration often cited arises when a child is recognised as being so far in advance of pupils of their own age that they are fully capable of being placed in a Year 10 or Year 11 class and encouraged to take a Religious Studies GCSE examination, or some other form of national accreditation, several years before the normal age of sixteen.

## Part-time acceleration

Acceleration is usually a permanent arrangement. Temporary or part-time acceleration may involve taking a very able child who shows a high level of competence and interest in a particular topic and placing them with an older class where they are taught that topic for a short period of time. For example, a Year 7 able child who shows an interest in science and religion may be placed with a Year 9 class that are exploring the topic of science and religion for perhaps two or three lessons. Following the experience the child returns to their normal class in Year 7.

## Is acceleration a good idea?

Acceleration is often promoted by organisations like NAGC (National Association for Gifted Children) and by parents who do not believe that exceptionally able young people can be accommodated in classrooms which put children together based on chronological age. An RE department may decide on an early entry policy for students who are thought to be able to successfully take the Religious Studies GCSE exam early. Or a department may decide that acceleration is the right policy in some cases and that it should not be ruled out of consideration.

The only serious research work on acceleration in British schools was undertaken by Joan Freeman (2001). She studied the progress of 210 young people of whom 140 were very able over a period of some 25 years between the years 1974 and 2001. She interviewed them first when they were aged between 11 and 15 years, then again when they were aged about 23 or 28 and then again at the age of around 35 or 39. Of the 140 very able young people in the study, 17 of them had been accelerated.

The main finding was that although two of the seventeen at the time thought acceleration was a good idea, 25 years later even they had decided it had not been good for them in the long run. Twenty-five years after the experience there was no discernable academic advantage for young people who had been accelerated, when compared with other young people who had not been accelerated.

Indeed some reported resentment claiming that at the time, 'having to make relationships every day with classmates who were emotionally more mature was confusing and also aggravated relationships at home' (Freeman, p. 217). The report also suggested that acceleration may have had a more lasting negative impact making it difficult for many of those who had been accelerated to establish fully rounded lives as adults. In her study Joan Freeman comments, 'It can only be concluded that unless a pupil is not only highly gifted but mature for his or her years, school acceleration is probably not the best option.'

Other research data published in 2004 entitled *A Nation Deceived*, mainly undertaken in America and Germany, contradicts Joan Freeman's conclusions. It concludes that 'acceleration is one of the most effective curriculum interventions for many high-ability learners'.

Given the uncertain nature of the research data available Joan Freeman's conclusions have to be considered as tentative. However, they are particularly pertinent in a subject like RE where academic progress alone would not be considered to be a satisfactory goal if it were at the expense of personal and social development. It is also the case that some topics which are often explored in RE lessons have a social and emotional content which makes them relevant for older adolescents but unsuitable for younger children. For example, a discussion about abortion or how you should conduct yourself in a relationship with a member of the opposite sex, taking into account various religious and moral arguments, might seem appropriate with a class of fifteen-year-olds. It is not at all clear that this would be a suitable diet for a twelve-year-old who had been accelerated into the class on the basis of their high academic skills.

As part of its policy an RE department may decide not to entirely rule out acceleration. Instead it may decide to use acceleration only sparingly in exceptional circumstances and only where pupils are socially very secure. In addition the department may agree that the situation should be monitored closely to ensure that the policy is not having any adverse effects.

## Listening to the child

Central to the teaching of RE is the idea of giving children a voice in the classroom. RE is not simply learning about religion; it is also giving children the opportunities and skills to form and express their own views. Alongside this of course there must be a willingness to listen to what children have to say.

The willingness to listen to children is also an important ingredient when teaching children who are gifted. Listening to the child involves taking seriously what children have to say about what interests them and about how they wish to extend their own learning. In an RE department this would involve adopting an approach where there are at least some opportunities for children to pursue a more personalised programme of work. With such an approach pupils can identify topics which they wish to look at in more depth or explore areas of minority interest which intrigue them and about which they wish to know more.

A very able child, indeed even children that find learning difficult, may develop a lively interest in any one of a number of different topics, for example:

- attitudes to women within the Christian Church

- the impact of the teaching of Mawlana Maududi on Islam in the twentieth century

- Krishna and the Bhakti tradition in Hinduism

- the development of the belief in Angels in Judaism and Christianity

- Christian attitudes to animal rights

- Jewish responses to the Holocaust

- TV evangelism in America

- the concept of Buddha in the Mahayana Tradition

- growing up as a Sikh in Britain today

- the Passover Plot Argument

- Christianity and the music of U2

- religion on British TV

- New Age Spirituality – does it make sense?

Allowing children to identify what they find most interesting and giving them an opportunity to follow that interest might be part of a deliberate policy an RE department chooses to adopt.

## A learning mentor

To support such a policy a department might encourage some very able children to use a learning mentor. A learning mentor might be the child's own RE teacher, or it might be another member of the department, or perhaps a member of staff from outside the RE department. The role of the learning mentor is simply to meet regularly with the child, say every three weeks or so, and discuss with them their learning, how they feel they are making progress, what they are currently interested in, whether anything is impeding their progress, whether there are particular resources they need help in accessing, whether the school or the department could be doing anything more or anything differently which they would find helpful. A good learning mentor will also be able to suggest to pupils how they might take their learning forward directing them towards questions and ideas to be considered, or suggesting to them books, films, websites and other sources of information they might like to explore.

A learning mentor programme can provide real insights into how able children may be responding to the education they are receiving and can help prevent problems which can hinder progress from arising in the first place. It can also help young people think more seriously about their own progress and take more responsibility for their learning. It can, however, be quite a drain on a precious resource – teachers' time. Meetings with a learning mentor need not be one-to-one, indeed such arrangements raise issues around child protection. A learning mentor might meet with two or three pupils together. Nevertheless, with limited workforce time available, the numbers that might benefit from a learning mentor might be relatively small.

## Learning diaries

Learning diaries also help children to get more involved in directing their own learning but can usually be used to engage more students than is the case with learning mentors. A learning diary involves students keeping a record of their learning in RE. A learning diary is, however, more than a list of topics studied in RE lessons. A learning diary should also contain a student's ideas, comments, thoughts and reflections. Following a lesson a question may occur to a student. This should be recorded in their learning diary and, if possible, followed up later perhaps with their RE teacher or maybe through personal research.

Some very able students are voracious readers. A learning diary may contain a record of books, websites and articles a student has read together with an account of some of the main ideas or information they gained from particular sources. Or a student may choose to write in their diary a brief review of what they thought of the book or article or include a note about other books or authors they should read, or at least find out more about.

A learning diary may contain a brief account of a discussion a student has with a group of friends or a member of the family outside of school. During the discussion certain claims may have been made or arguments asserted. These may be recorded in the learning diary so that they can be considered and thought over at length.

Through the use of a learning diary young people can be encouraged to develop a much more systematic and rigorous approach to their learning so that their knowledge and thinking acquires more depth and substance. It can encourage in young people good practice and a lifetime habit of developing their learning in an organised and directed way. This is not to rule out haphazard, random learning and the joys of serendipity. However, in RE as in all other areas of study, young people should be helped to appreciate that a much greater level of understanding and insight can be achieved if knowledge and ideas are followed through and tested under the scrutiny of critical reflection.

## Summary

- An RE department that has a G&T policy usually enjoys success with very able pupils.

- A G&T policy should emerge from an informed, professional discussion.

- The progress of more able pupils is a job for everyone in the RE team.

- The commitment to effective teaching of able pupils should be supported through subject leadership.

- For effective learning pupils need to be known as individuals.

# CHAPTER 3

# Recognising high ability and potential in RE

- Why identify the very able in RE?
- Five main sources of information
- Characteristics of being gifted in RE
- Learning about and learning from religion
- The concept of 'understanding' in RE
- Breadth of knowledge
- Depth of knowledge
- Academic disciplines and depth

## Why identify the very able in RE?

Most schools today are expected to draw up a list of the young people who they teach who are the most able in RE so that they might be included in a school's gifted and talented register.

The reason for having a gifted and talented register is because it is false to assume that schools don't have to do much to help very able children make progress in school. The assumption has been that a young person who is gifted in RE can more or less fend for themselves. A very able pupil need do little more than show up for the lessons and 'do the work' and success will be the outcome. This is an illusion. Some very able young people will make good progress in RE despite the fact that very little extra is undertaken in the classroom to help them. However, unlike corks, some very able pupils do not naturally rise to the top. They need nurturing, guidance and targeted support. To ensure that this happens it is of great help if they are identified so that they are not simply lost in the system and allowed to drift. Instead they are directed and systematically supported to ensure that whatever potential they show in the subject is realised.

## Personalised learning

This does not mean that additional resources or time are taken away from other pupils and directed at pupils gifted in RE in some sort of elitist programme. It does mean, however, that there is an increasing realisation that each child needs a more personalised education which is tailored to his/her particular requirements. Just as a child who has a difficulty with reading has special needs, so also a child who is gifted in RE has special needs which have to be addressed through a programme which is more personalised to meet those needs.

## Identifying pupils gifted in RE

Within RE there is often a tendency to treat the subject as being mystically unique, claiming that it is unlike other subjects taught in the school curriculum. Because of RE's special nebulous qualities, it is claimed, identifying pupils gifted in the subject is a shrouded business more akin to an art than a science. Such claims are often overexaggerated and they should not be used as an excuse for not effectively trying to identify those pupils who are most able in RE.

## Five main sources of information

In order to identify very able pupils in RE, teachers do not have to introduce time-consuming additional tasks or special testing procedures. There are five main sources of information available which are likely to reveal the main candidates for an RE G&T register. These are:

- SATs and standardised test scores

- primary school recommendation

- subject teacher nomination

- parent nomination

- pupil and peer nomination.

## SATs and standardised test scores

On entry into a school most secondary school teachers of RE have available to them the SATs results of the pupils they teach. Teachers of RE would be unwise to ignore these SATs results on the grounds that the identification of pupils in RE should be based on distinct RE knowledge, skills and understanding. Of course it is true that SATs results identify those pupils who have a high level of ability in English, maths and science. Having a high level of ability in these core subjects does not necessarily coincide with having ability in RE. Nevertheless, the general skills a young person needs to have, particularly in English, are likely to serve a person well in RE, for example the ability to:

- comprehend and use language effectively

- grasp ideas

- acquire and retain knowledge

- recognise differences

- identify similarities.

Of course it is perfectly possible for a young person to be outstanding in English, maths and science and yet be little more than average, or even poor in RE. However, this would be extremely unusual. Indeed, if a child did have very high SATs scores but in the classroom demonstrated only mediocre skills in RE, alarm bells should be ringing. In such a case the RE department should be asking serious questions about why a very able child appears not to be performing well in RE, for example:

- is there a reason why the child may be underachieving in RE?

- is the work in RE unchallenging and so fails to identify young people of outstanding ability?

- is the child performing well in RE but is doing so in a way that the department has failed to recognise?

- does the child have potential in the subject which has yet to be realised?

## Standardised test scores

In addition to SATs many schools have available to them additional information about the pupils they teach based on test results. By far the most popular of these are the NFER CAT tests (cognitive ability tests). These are tests in what are described as three areas of reasoning – verbal reasoning, non-verbal reasoning and numerical reasoning.

As with SATs, standardised scores if available should not be ignored by teachers of RE as being irrelevant to the particular knowledge, skills and understanding RE seeks to develop. It is perfectly possible for a child to have a high cognitive test score and yet show no flair for RE. However, a high cognitive test score but low performance in the RE classroom should alert teachers to the possibility that something may be wrong. Wide discrepancy between a child's test scores and classroom performance should trigger closer scrutiny to find out if there is a problem, for example, inaccurate teacher assessment or pupil underachievement.

Often the results of the NFER verbal, non-verbal and numerical tests are combined together and averaged giving a single numerical figure for each child. An RE G&T coordinator who may be scrutinising these figures needs to be wary if this is happening. Some pupils can have high non-verbal reasoning scores and may have the potential to be exceptional in RE. However, their verbal or numerical reasoning scores may be quite low resulting in an unremarkable average when the three scores are amalgamated. A child with a high non-verbal reasoning score may, with proper training and support, have the potential to do well in RE. However, this potential may be overlooked as attention is being given to the child's unimpressive combined test score.

## Primary school recommendation

Many primary schools have a G&T register of the very able pupils they teach. It is not unreasonable to expect that by the end of Year 6 a primary school will have identified pupils who are exceptional in RE and that this assessment can be passed on to the secondary school which the child enters in Year 7.

That does not mean of course that an assessment made in a primary school that a child is gifted in RE is irrevocable and must stand forever. It is simply to suggest that secondary teachers of RE should accord due respect to their primary colleagues. If a primary teacher believes that a child who they have taught over a period of time has a gift for RE this assessment should be taken seriously and should not be simply dismissed or ignored.

When a teacher of RE meets a Year 7 class for the first time in September they need not be confronted by 29 or 30 young individuals about whom they know nothing. By drawing upon SATs, CATs and primary transmission information a teacher should already have a rough idea of some of the pupils to keep an eye out for who may be very able in RE and who are provisional candidates, at least, for the school's or department's G&T register.

### Primary and secondary collaboration

In the real world there are, however, practical difficulties. Many secondary schools complain that they have twenty or more primary feeder schools and that gathering G&T data from so many schools is not realistic. Electronic G&T registers and software pupil tracking systems may help schools to overcome the logistics of handling so much individual data about pupils.

However, even if such systems are not in place there is no reason why an RE G&T coordinator cannot take some initial cautionary steps and begin by contacting the RE coordinator in two or three of their main feeder schools. If secondary RE teachers find that their primary colleagues have made little progress identifying pupils who are very able in RE, such initial enquiries should not be regarded as a fruitless waste of time. Secondary and primary colleagues could agree to collaborate by drawing up a simple RE G&T criteria or checklist.

### An RE G&T checklist

An RE G&T checklist should not be overcomplicated. It should be based on the assessment advice and end of Key Stage statements or levels found in the local authority's agreed syllabus. If such information does not exist in the local agreed syllabus, colleagues may find the level descriptions in *The Non-Statutory National Framework for Religious Education* (DFES/QCA 2004) a helpful starting point. Enquiries may reveal that other schools in the authority or perhaps the authority's RE adviser, if one exists, may have already or is willing to help draft such criteria. An RE G&T checklist of ten key indicators which a primary teacher of RE could make use of might look something like the following:

| | RE G&T primary checklist | Evidence |
|---|---|---|
| 1. | Ask interesting and provocative questions related to religion and life, e.g. *'How can God be everywhere, Miss?' 'Do pets go to heaven?'* | |
| 2. | Recall fairly accurately religious stories. | |
| 3. | Give fairly accurate descriptions of religious festivals, ceremonies and rituals. | |
| 4. | Can understand and make use of specialist religious language. | |
| 5. | Are able to avoid confusing different religious traditions. | |
| 6. | Recognise similarities and differences between religions. | |
| 7. | Suggest a meaning or message within a religious story or suggest how a message in a story may have application in the world today. | |
| 8. | Often show a perceptive insight into why festivals, ceremonies, rituals or symbols are important in the lives of people today. | |
| 9. | Can talk about their own personal views related to religion and life and are able to support their views with coherent reasons. | |
| 10. | Engage very effectively in RE discussions and debates in the classroom. | |

Such a checklist should not be used like an MOT test so that all the boxes have to be ticked. It simply provides some of the broad characteristics which may suggest pupils who are very able in RE.

## Subject teacher nomination

National test scores and primary school nomination can be used to do a lot of the initial investigation when attempting to identify pupils who are very able. However, these two strategies alone are not sufficient. An additional strategy that must be used is subject teacher nomination. This involves conscious talent spotting by teachers of RE. They have to be always on the lookout for very able pupils in their classrooms who have not yet been recognised. To identify very able pupils who do not obviously stand out the teacher of RE has to set aside certain distractions and stereotypes. For example, pupils who are gifted at RE may:

● not be good all-rounders

● have poor writing skills

● have a short attention span

● be on the special needs register

● be keen to disguise their abilities.

### Not good all-rounders

Many very able pupils in RE are good at a number of other subjects as well. That is why SATs and CATs results can be used to provide initial pointers for pupils who are gifted in RE. However, it is possible for a pupil to be a high achiever in only RE and yet may be no more than average or well below average in all of their other subjects. Religious education may pose questions which have a particular fascination and personal relevance for some pupils. The subject may motivate and stimulate some pupils in such a way that it draws from them a level of effort and insight which simply does not show itself when they undertake other subjects. Because of this it is important to give weight to what a pupil does in RE and not to be too distracted by the unfavourable reports of other subject teachers.

### Poor writing skills

A child may be gifted in RE and yet may have very poor writing skills. Secondary teachers of RE often require pupils to express their thoughts and show their knowledge, skills and understanding by undertaking various written assignments and tasks. While this may help many pupils who find the more reflective and more private world of writing suits them, this is not true of all very able pupils. Some pupils are genuinely inhibited when asked to write and either avoid the task or commit only the minimum to paper.

Aversion to writing in pupils who have outstanding ability in RE may be due to a wide variety of reasons. For example, some pupils may have very poor spelling skills and so avoid writing as their experience has been that this exposes them to ridicule or failure. Some pupils are cognitively so active that when set a task, which others may see as black or white or relatively straightforward, they may see an array of different shades of grey and complex responses which require substantial reflection, all of which given the nature of the task and the time available cannot be committed to paper. Their cognitive reach is further than their communication grasp. Teachers may find that behind poor handwriting, scruffy or unintelligible work, poor spelling, failure to complete or even undertake assignments, there may be a child who is highly gifted. Alternatively, it is easy to mistake work as of high quality when on closer examination it is little more than neat, tidy, decorative and correct.

### Short attention span

It is also a mistake to assume that very able children in RE are always alert and attentive. The idea that a very able child is fixated on learning, is always compliant, cooperative, responsive to questions and anxious to do well is a myth. Ofsted has often reported that in Key Stage 3 RE often lacks challenge. All too many RE assignments require little more than recall, description, single word or short phrase answers, for example, 'What is the holy book of Islam called?' or 'Write an account of what happens during infant baptism.' In some cases pupils are being asked to repeat assignments which they undertook in Key Stage 2 (Wintersgill, 2000). Far from being engaged, a very able child may simply daydream, look out of the window, fidget, doodle in the back of their exercise book or generate a more interesting environment by engaging in low level, or even more serious disruptive behaviour. Recognising high ability in RE is not the same as recognising the most compliant, the most well-behaved or the most cooperative.

### Special needs register

A very able child in RE can be on both the special needs register and on a school's or department's G&T register. Having dyslexia, dyspraxia, Asperger syndrome or emotional behaviour disorder (EBD) are not incompatible with being gifted in RE. Some highly gifted children live in traumatic, angry homes and they bring their experience of anger with them into the classroom. Not surprisingly their gifted nature is cloaked by challenging and aggressive outbursts.

### Keen to disguise their abilities

Many children who are highly gifted in RE make a conscious effort not to shine in class. They do not put their hands up to ask or answer questions. During discussions they remain silent. Even when prompted their response may be evasive or halting. For example, during a Year 9 circle time discussion on near-death experiences the teacher asked if such experiences provided evidence of life after death. In the class many pupils expressed their view but when Dylan was asked his only response was to shrug his shoulders and say, 'It's possible.' The teacher appeared to accept this answer and moved on to the more forthcoming responses of other pupils. However, when all the other pupils had expressed their view the teacher returned to Dylan and encouraged him to add more to his initial 'It's possible' response. Dylan started slowly, but as he got into his stride he said: 'Medical research suggests that when parts of the brain became short of oxygen, as can happen during a near-death experience, brain cells start to go wrong. This could give rise to the mistaken belief that you are dead. It could also cause illusions. These illusions could resemble the experiences people near to death were describing.'

Pupils may disguise their abilities because there is not an effective ethos in the school which encourages high achievement. Some children simply do not feel that it is 'cool to be clever' in RE or any other subject and that doing well in school mars their 'street cred' and alienates them from their peers. Not standing out is more comfortable. However, behind the shrugged shoulders, the 'don't know', and the 'it's possible' answers there may be a highly informed and active mind which with the right promptings may be encouraged to show itself.

## Characteristics of being gifted in RE

In RE in order to be able to identify the more able pupil it is important to be clear about the characteristics of a pupil who is gifted in RE and not confuse them with other qualities a child may show. It is perfectly possible for a pupil to be highly exceptional in RE but have no religious faith at all. Indeed they may even be sharply critical, even hostile to religion and yet still be outstanding in RE. Take the case, for example, of Stephen.

### Case example 1 – A child gifted in RE: Stephen Year 8

Stephen is often critical, sometimes hostile, towards all religious traditions. He says believing in God is a childish idea like believing in Father Christmas. He retains information with ease but he shows little interest in the factual detail of religious practices or ceremonies. He has a detailed and comprehensive grasp of religious beliefs and ideas, particularly Christianity, Islam and Buddhism.

Stephen has an excellent command of language and often invents similes, analogies and metaphors to express himself in discussion and in written RE assignments. When talking about prayer he suggested:

'Prayer must be like having your own therapist. In prayer not only is there the feeling that God speaks to you. Just as important there is the comfort of knowing that in God there is always someone there who is patiently listening.'

Stephen doesn't so much give descriptive accounts of what happens in religion. Instead he is more inclined to give an analysis seeking to explain why a religious symbol or ceremony is so important. For example, in a discussion about Holy Communion Stephen suggested that the bread was:

'. . . not like normal bread which gives you physical energy. It's like spiritual bread which gives Christians the spiritual energy they need to live a Christian life.'

Even though Stephen doesn't have a faith himself he has a thoughtful insight into the psychology of faith and is able to put into words how having a religion may be a source of peace and security. For example, in an assignment on zakat, the Islamic requirement on every Muslim to give 2.5% of their disposable income to those who are poor, Stephen wrote:

'Zakat tells you exactly what you have to give. Instead of being anxious wondering if you have given enough or always thinking, "Should I have done more?" Islam takes away that worry by spelling out just what you have to do. Instead of being in doubt, Islam offers certainty.'

When expressing his own opinion his written work often engages the reader by the use of rhetorical questions and attempts to identify logical inconsistencies. For example, when exploring the idea of God he asked, 'If God made the world, who made God?'

In another assignment he shows an ability to write a reasoned argument which retains a logical thread through several sentences, for example:

'I can't believe in a God who would send people to hell. If God made everything then he must have also made hell. Why would a loving God do that? By creating hell, God is adding more evil into the universe, not making the universe less evil.'

Stephen does refer to alternative points of view and arguments to the contrary. When he does so he is not dismissive. Frequently he expresses understanding, for example, in a discussion about what happens after death he commented, 'It must be nice to believe in life after death. I mean . . . nobody really wants to die.'

Effective teacher nomination of very able pupils in RE depends on teachers not relying on single pieces of evidence like classroom test scores or assessment assignments. As was the case with the primary RE checklist, teachers should make use of a wider body of evidence by being alert to:

- questions which young people ask in the classroom

- verbal responses to questions, tasks, visiting speakers, visits

- contributions to class discussions and debates

- classroom written assignments

- homework assignments

- level of interest and attitude in the classroom.

## Potential high ability

Teachers should not only be trying to identify the most able pupils in RE, they should also be trying to spot those pupils who have the potential to be high achievers but are not yet demonstrating that potential. To do this sometimes teachers may have to make an initial decision on what is little more than a hunch. A child may catch a teacher's eye by:

- leaning forward during a challenging part of a lesson appearing to be particularly alert

- showing an intense but silent interest in a religious artefact as it is passed round the room

- making a whispered but thoughtful aside to a classmate

- hanging back at the end of a lesson to ask a question or to enquire about books or websites they could look at to follow up on the RE lesson.

Teachers are often sensitive to such signs. They stand out as unusual. As empirical data they are not sufficient to persuade other colleagues that a child is gifted, nevertheless it is important that teachers of RE are sensitive to such signs and follow up on their hunches. For example, following a hunch a teacher may make a deliberate effort to note more formally what the pupil does during the lessons. By doing so the teacher may find that they develop a body of evidence so that their initial hunch becomes a substantiated judgement. As could be seen in the case example of Stephen, secondary RE teachers should not be simply looking for young people who know a lot about the different religions being studied. Essentially the teacher should be on the lookout for young people who are thoughtful and show discernment and insight rather than mere knowledge.

Not unlike the primary RE G&T checklist for pupils, a secondary checklist might look something like the following. It will, however, alter depending on the requirements of the local agreed syllabus.

| | RE G&T secondary checklist | Example | Evidence |
|---|---|---|---|
| 1. | Ask interesting and provocative questions related to religion and life. | *'If Jesus saved us from evil why is there still evil in the world?' 'Why is religion often involved in so many conflicts around the world?'* | |
| 2. | Draw upon a knowledge of religious beliefs to explain why rituals and ceremonies and other forms of religious behaviour have significance in the lives of people today. | *'The Sabbath is a day set aside every week for not working but for doing the things that make us fully human. A wild animal has to hunt for food every day but the Sabbath is when we don't do what the other animals do. Instead we can do the things that make us more human.'* | |
| 3. | Show an awareness of how psychological, social, moral, theological or philosophical factors may be of significance when explaining why rituals, ceremonies and other forms of religious behaviour may have significance in the lives of people today. | *'By worshipping at the same time, in the same way and in the same direction, prayer helps Muslims to feel spiritually bonded together as a global community.'* | |
| 4. | Understand diversity within religious traditions and that faith may be a holistic view or may be based on a narrative about the world which gives meaning. | *'Christians believe that in some way the relationship between God and humans had become broken. In order to restore that broken relationship God had to enter into the world . . .'* | |

| | RE G&T secondary checklist | Example | Evidence |
|---|---|---|---|
| 5. | Are able to analyse religious responses to contemporary moral issues by discussing a range of sources rather than rely on single propositions taken from scripture. | *'The principle which runs through the Qur'an is that human nature is often wayward. Humans must have fixed and very clear rules or else they will go off the straight path.'* | |
| 6. | Show awareness of how religious belief and practice may have application in the world today. | *'By fasting a person may become genuinely aware of what hunger is like and so be much more motivated to do something to help those who are poor or hungry.'* | |
| 7. | Are able to express their own personal views about religion and life and are able to defend their view by sustaining a reasoned argument through which runs a consistent logical thread. | *'I do not think that beautiful things in the world necessarily means that there is a God. I feel like this because not everything is perfectly designed. For example, a deformed baby may give rise to a difficult life for the child and those who know it. This hardly seems to be the work of a loving designer God.'* | |
| 8. | Show awareness of arguments to the contrary, or weaknesses in their own line of reasoning, and are able to provide a coherent defence of their own views. | *'Some people feel that there is a God that designed the world. They may believe that there is no other explanation for things such as rainbows and the human eye. I don't agree with this because the creation of most things can be scientifically explained, such as the rainbow made by water droplets and sunlight.'* | |
| 9. | Use a balanced and discursive tone avoiding emotive or disrespectful language. | *'This is not a straightforward issue for which there is one neat answer . . .'* | |

| | RE G&T secondary checklist | Example | Evidence |
|---|---|---|---|
| 10. | Are able to defend their point of view using a range of rhetorical devices including analogy, narrative, rhetorical questions, empirical evidence, identifying reasonable consequences and are usually able to avoid false conclusions based upon generalised claims from insufficient evidence, stereotyping, ambiguities of language and false premises. | *'When we die we pass into eternal life. A caterpillar changes into a completely different but much more beautiful life as a butterfly. So also when we die, it is possible, there is a much more beautiful life on the other side.'* | |

## 'Religiously gifted'

A child may be devout; in other words they may have a strong religious faith, but this is not the same as being gifted in RE. Being gifted in RE is not the same as being 'religiously gifted'. Consider the following example:

### Case example 2 – A devout child: Karen Year 7

Karen has a strong faith commitment. She is an active member of a local church. She has a real sense of the presence of the Holy Spirit in her life. Karen has an excellent knowledge of Christian practices, rituals and festivals. Her Bible knowledge, particularly of Bible stories, is very good. She has a very good grasp of Christian terminology and makes use of words like 'Christ', 'Holy Communion', 'the Holy Spirit' and 'resurrection'.

Karen is very keen to talk about her faith and frequently makes statements like 'As a Christian, I feel as if Jesus is alive and with me every day of my life.' However, she undertakes little analysis of her faith. When asked about the significance or purpose of religious practices she uses a limited number of repeated responses like:

'Prayer makes me feel closer to God.'

'Easter is very special.'

'The Bible is important because it is the Christians' holy book.'

When pressed as to what she means when she says, 'It's holy' or 'It's special' or 'feel closer to God' she is unable to elaborate, indicating that these phrases are little more than clichés which disguise real understanding.

Karen similarly shows a familiarity with particularly Christian theological statements like:

'Jesus is the Son of God.'

'The Bread symbolises the Body of Christ.'

'The Trinity is the Father, the Son and the Holy Spirit.'

However, when given opportunities to expand on what these statements mean she often merely repeats the same words or inconsequentially changes the grammar,

'. . . it means Jesus is God's Son'. Her lack of understanding of these statements suggests that these are little more than learnt formulaic responses the meaning of which Karen has not grasped.

As well as Christianity Karen has a positive attitude to other religions but her knowledge and understanding of other religions is similar to many other members of the class. She has a respectful response to other religions as she believes that they all share something in common, a belief in a transcendent God. She sees them as being mutual allies who believe in God and help give her confidence in a materialistic world which she feels often ignores God and doesn't take belief seriously.

Karen is actively friendly, helpful and courteous towards friends and strangers alike. She is invariably upbeat and positive. She is helpful and supportive of other children who are unpopular or marginalised.

Karen as a devout or a pious child may be described as 'religiously gifted' as her particular faith community might recognise a child's gifts. However, she is not 'gifted' in the sense in which the word 'gifted' is used when talking about the education of gifted and talented young people.

Although she has an excellent knowledge of Christian ceremonies, rituals and festivals which enables her to give accurate descriptive accounts of what Christians do, her understanding of these rituals which would enable her to explain why these rituals have significance in Christianity remains as yet little more than rudimentary. The distinction between the 'when, how and who' knowledge as opposed to 'why' knowledge is crucial in religious education. When exploring religious behaviour, young people gifted in RE tend to ask 'why' questions and they tend to give informed answers to 'why' questions. In other words they seek to explain religious phenomena and not simply describe it.

### Gifted with a moral or social conscience

Another characteristic which is often mistaken as an indication of being gifted in RE is that of a pupil with a strong moral or social conscience. For example, consider the following case:

### Case example 3 – A child with a social conscience: Jackie Year 8

Jackie is an active member of her local church. She has been involved in a variety of church activities including a visit to Walsingham and raising money for children in Romania.

She currently is attending confirmation classes. She has an excellent factual knowledge of Christianity. She is familiar with a large number of Bible stories and is able to quote passages frequently from the Gospels. For example, she intersperses her classroom contributions with statements like 'You cannot love both God and money' and 'Jesus said, "Treat other people as you would have them treat you."'

Jackie generally has a cautious response to religions other than Christianity but her knowledge and understanding is not substantially different from other children in the class. When asked about the significance or purpose of religious practices

> Jackie nearly always provides an answer based on religious authority. For example, when asked to explain why Baptism is undertaken Jackie suggested: 'Because it's in the Bible.' When asked about the value or purpose of prayer Jackie volunteered the answer: 'Prayer is very special. Jesus prayed a lot.'
>
> Jackie is often outspoken in class on moral and social issues. When expressing her own opinion she speaks and writes passionately, often using emotive language. During a discussion of world poverty she announced, 'People die every day in Africa because they don't have clean water. It's terrible!' On another occasion when discussing animal rights Jackie said, 'It's just not right. Have you seen those poor little rabbits that get experimented on?' She never refers to alternative points of view or arguments to the contrary.
>
> Jackie is an active member of the RSPCA, Christian Aid and Amnesty. She has some experience of campaigning including organising a petition about the school's uniform and attending a peace rally in London.

Jackie has a clear sense of right and wrong and is so highly motivated on certain issues that she is willing to engage in social action. For many people, all of this is highly commendable. In most RE schemes of work there are to be found inspirational men and women like Mother Teresa, Martin Luther King, Jackie Pullinger and Mohandas Gandhi. The lives of such people are made known to young people not simply so that they might learn how religion may impact on a person's life. The lives of such people are seen as suitable models from whom young people may be inspired to live their own life in a way which is not narrowly self-serving but which aspires to something nobler.

It cannot be denied that encouraging young people to have moral awareness and a social conscience are qualities RE seeks to achieve. However, if a young person had these social qualities but had only average ability when it comes to insight, understanding and analysis of religion, it would not be appropriate to describe them as very able in RE.

Although Jackie has an excellent factual knowledge of Christianity and of the Bible, she doesn't show a distinctively high level of understanding of Christianity in terms of its teachings or its ceremonies. When she expresses her opinions and views she uses reasons which rely on religious authority like statements in the Bible and the example of Jesus. These are all very well as long as she is only trying to persuade an audience which accepts these sources as having authority. However, a very able pupil could be expected to make use of reasons which would appeal to a wider audience. Also, a very able pupil could be expected to make less use of emotive language and make more use of a balanced and discursive tone anticipating arguments to the contrary and attempting to address them.

### Being 'spiritually gifted'

Some young people have a natural spiritual gift. However, as is the case with a pupil with a strong social conscience, being spiritually gifted would not in itself be a sufficient characteristic feature of a child gifted in RE. The following is an example of a pupil who is spiritually gifted.

## Case example 4 – A child who is spiritually gifted: Imram Year 9

Imram has no direct connections with any organised religion. He has a tolerant, easy-going attitude and generally respects the fact that people's ideas and beliefs may differ.

He has an above average factual knowledge of several religions particularly Christianity, Sikhism and Islam. When asked about the significance or purpose of religious practices and ceremonies he tends to identify social and moral factors. For example, in a passage describing the hajj he wrote, 'Going on pilgrimage is really important. At Makkah Muslims have a sense of brotherhood.' Following a visit to a gurdwara, Imram commented, 'I liked the Langar most. Everybody was so friendly and everybody was treated equally.'

During RE lessons Imram is often quiet and only volunteers answers or shares his views when directly asked. He is liked and admired by his peers and has been known to take a lead in situations of potential conflict by calming things down, reconciling differences and speaking quietly to people to get them to see reason.

When expressing his own point of view Imram is always courteous and respectful. He is often very still and reflective. He has a keen sense of his own values and beliefs which he expresses without resorting to emotive language. During a discussion about what they valued most Imram commented, 'Family and friends are really important. Even if you had a million pounds it doesn't always make you happy.' Imram is even-tempered and has a strong sense of right and wrong. He does refer to other points of view and arguments to the contrary.

Although Imram is rich when it comes to personal, spiritual and moral gifts, he does not show the knowledge, skills or understanding associated with being gifted in RE.

So far we have considered three important sources of information that may be used when identifying pupils who are very able in RE. There remain two more sources of information which are not to be ignored. These are parent nomination and peer nomination.

## Parent nomination

Unless a problem arises parents are often left on the fringes of education and are not effectively consulted about their own children. Yet parents see their children at close quarters and in less formal circumstances than teachers do. They are more likely than most teachers of RE, who have a responsibility for many children, to know what their own child reads, talks about, shows an interest in and has an understanding of.

Because of this, schools should encourage parents not to regard the flow of information about their children as being a one-way street passing only from schools to parents. Information needs to flow in both directions so that parents who have something they wish to discuss or report about their child should feel that their school encourages and welcomes this. If a parent reports, perhaps to the form teacher or to the RE teacher, that their child may be gifted in RE, such a report should not be ignored but should be given due weight and explored further.

It is of course possible that a parent's love and aspirations for their child can lead to an inflated judgement. Parents do sometimes believe that they can see exceptional ability in their children when a more professional and disinterested judgement would be that the child is no more than able or perhaps even average. It is of course also possible that a parent may not understand the nature of RE. They may regard a child who has a strong interest in church activities or is able to recall off by heart large sections of the Qur'an as being sufficient evidence of being gifted in RE. Parents, like teachers, can get it wrong. Nevertheless, a wise teacher of RE would do well to look more closely at a child declared by their parent to be gifted.

## Peer nomination

Just as parents see their own children in close and intimate ways, so also children encounter each other and learn about their peers in ways which may not be available to teachers of RE. Through daily encounters, children learn who in their midst are natural leaders, who amongst them are listened to and whose words are noted and have authority.

Sometimes in an RE classroom it is possible to witness young people encouraging an individual to step out of the shadows and take a prominent role which may involve speaking on behalf of a group or giving a lead on an assignment. Occasionally in conversation with children they make references to, or even directly name, another child and it is clear from their comments that they believe that a particular child has a capacity in RE that commands their respect. Children can be well aware that another child may be acting as the classroom clown, putting in a performance of bravado, or affecting to be bored. However, in reality in the playground, or after school in the library, or at a friend's house playing on the PC, this is the person they talk to about issues which are of real substance related to life, religion, and right and wrong. This is the person they talk to when they can't do their RE homework or if something comes up in the RE lesson which they don't understand and which they want to sort out.

The teacher of RE needs to be alert to what children say about each other. If an individual is named by a child, or several children, or even by the child themselves as being a 'boffin in RE', as with parent nomination, such comments should be followed up to see if there is evidence which just hasn't been noticed and which can support the claim.

## Learning about religion and learning from religion

The specific nature of religious education in any maintained school must be taught in accordance with the locally agreed syllabus. This does give rise to some variations and differences in what teachers of RE are being asked to achieve. It also gives rise to some variations in what precisely they might be expected to look for when identifying highly able pupils in the subject.

However, over the last decade or so there has emerged a broad consensus about both the content and the aims of RE. Part of that consensus is that the subject has two main aims. These two aims are usually described as being *learning about religion* and *learning from religion.*

## Learning about religion

The first of these aims is that RE has an important role in helping young people to develop their knowledge and understanding of different religious traditions. There are plenty of different views about what exactly young people should be helped to know and understand about the different religious traditions. There are also differences about what should be the appropriate portion or balance accorded to the different religious traditions in a scheme of work. Nevertheless, it is generally agreed that RE should be involved in teaching young people to know and understand about the different world religions.

### Interpersonal intelligence

High achievement in *learning about religion* is often associated with young people who show, using Howard Gardner's original seven intelligence categories, interpersonal intelligence; that is they have the ability to get along with others as they show a high level of understanding of the motives and reasons which drive human behaviour. However, to be a high attainer at *learning about religion* a young person also has to be able to combine interpersonal intelligence with a high level of verbal–linguistic intelligence. Without a good command of language which enables a young person to translate their high level of understanding into a form that makes coherent sense to others, high attainment in the area of *learning about religion* is unlikely to be achieved.

It is sometimes claimed that a high level of understanding can be expressed through music, dance or art. In other words, a pupil may not have to have a high level of verbal–linguistic intelligence to express themselves so they may make use of music–rhythmic intelligence, bodily–kinaesthetic intelligence or spatial intelligence. However, it is not at all clear that this is really the case. Pupils may through art or music express their insight into the religious life of others but in order for others to understand what they may be saying through their chosen medium, nearly always pupils have to fall back on a linguistic commentary to explain what they mean.

## Learning from religion

The second aim, but by no means of any less importance, is that RE is also deeply involved in helping young people with their own personal development. The idea behind this aim is that through the study of religions, young people inevitably encounter rituals, ceremonies, teachings and beliefs which can challenge or inspire them to think about their own life. Religions make certain claims which are held to be true, for example, 'There is a God that created the universe', 'Each of us has a soul which survives our physical death', 'God may be known through God's revelation'. Naturally the study of religion raises questions like 'Are these claims really true?' 'Do I personally believe in these claims?' By being encouraged to confront and evaluate for themselves such truth-claims, young people in RE are involved in a programme of personal growth. This personal growth comes about as young people are encouraged to seek and become clear in their own minds about what they believe, what shapes their lives and what sort of values they identify with most which will form the core of their being. This does not mean that RE is about helping young people to find religion. It is, however, about helping young people to find answers to questions, and finding values and beliefs which give their life meaning. As George Eliot expressed it in the question asked by her heroine Dorothea in *Middlemarch*, 'What's your religion? I mean what's the belief that helps you most?'

## Intrapersonal intelligence

As was true with *learning about religion*, young people who have an exceptional ability in *learning from religion* almost without exception have a high level of verbal–linguistic intelligence. However, in terms of Gardner's multiple intelligences the principle requirement to do well at *learning from religion* is not interpersonal intelligence; it is intrapersonal intelligence. If a young person with interpersonal intelligence thrives on tasks which require the understanding of others, a person with intrapersonal intelligence has a high level of ability to engage in self-reflection, to explore what they think and to engage in tasks which require self-discovery.

Typically the learning style of pupils with intrapersonal intelligence is one of thriving on self-reliance and individual work. They do not respond well to too many teacher-directed activities but prefer having time to be left alone and to reflect. This contrasts with the learning style of pupils who have interpersonal intelligence. Such pupils typically dislike working alone. They prefer to work with others engaging in activities such as cooperative learning groups, role-play, team solving, and getting and giving feedback.

However, despite the differences in preferred learning styles, interpersonal and intrapersonal intelligence are not necessarily mutually exclusive. Both types of intelligence can reside in the same person.

## The Non-Statutory National Framework for Religious Education (NFRE)

*The Non-Statutory National Framework for Religious Education* (NFRE) reinforced this broad consensus that RE is best described in the form of two attainment targets. The framework describes *learning about religion* and *learning from religion* in the following terms:

> *Learning about religion* includes enquiry into, and investigation of, the nature of religion, its beliefs, teachings and ways of life, sources, practices and forms of expression. It includes the skills of interpretation, analysis and explanation. Pupils learn to communicate their knowledge and understanding using

specialist vocabulary. It also includes identifying and developing an understanding of ultimate questions and ethical issues. In the national framework, learning about religion covers pupils' knowledge and understanding of individual religions and how they relate to each other as well as the study of the nature and characteristics of religion.

*Learning from religion* is concerned with developing pupils' reflection on and response to their own and others' experiences in the light of their learning about religion. It develops pupils' skills of application, interpretation and evaluation of what they learn about religion. Pupils learn to develop and communicate their own ideas, particularly in relation to questions of identity and belonging, meaning, purpose and truth, and values and commitments.

(DFES/QCA 2004, p. 11)

*Learning about* and *learning from religion* are closely related, indeed in certain areas they effectively overlap. For example, imagine a lesson, or a series of lessons, about the story of Zacchaeus, the wealthy but dishonest tax-collector of Jericho. During the course of the work the pupils might be invited to think about what the story is telling us. Rather like a Gospel commentary young people might be invited to interpret the story. In answer to that question students may suggest the following answer:

## Answer A

The story tells us that Jesus cared about the outcast and the rejected. It tells us that Jesus believed that by reaching out, even to those who treat us badly, a person can be changed and become not our enemy but our friend.

Such an analysis of the text might be described as leading to a deeper understanding of Jesus' teaching and what Christianity is about. In other words, the lesson would primarily be focused on *learning about religion*, in this case, learning about the religion of Christianity.

But imagine the assignment were slightly different and instead of the students being asked, 'What does the story tell us?' the assignment had been, 'What can we learn from this story?' A student may offer the following answer:

## Answer B

The story tells us that if someone is horrible to you, like they push in front in the dinner queue. The next time you see them, say in the playground and they want to join in your game of football, instead of telling them to clear off you might let them join in. By letting them join in you get to know them better and they get to know you and so they stop being horrible.

An answer of this kind may be described as seeing how religious teaching may have an application in one's own life. In other words the child may have *learnt from religion* that returning bad-mannered behaviour with kindness may have an application in their own life. However, the skills involved in arriving at the two answers, Answer A and Answer B, that of interpreting religious text, are essentially the same.

The reason why it is important to be familiar with RE's two attainment targets is because as has already been noted the specific type of intelligence a person is likely to have to achieve a high level of attainment is not identical in the two targets and so not all pupils are gifted in both targets. Consider the following example:

## Case example 5 – Gifted in learning about religion: Shapla Year 9

Shapla is a highly motivated student who has acquired an active interest in the phenomenon of religion. She is able to describe in impressive detail the major festivals, rituals, ceremonies, forms of worship, beliefs and doctrines associated with a variety of religious traditions particularly Islam, Christianity and Sikhism.

As well as being able to describe rituals and ceremonies she is often able to give a subtle and highly informed account of what faith or a ritual may mean from the point of view of the believer. For example, in one assignment Shapla avoided a descriptive account of Mother Teresa's life but instead attempted to explain how her Christian faith inspired her work. She wrote:

'When she helps a destitute that has a face disfigured by leprosy she looks into that destitute's face and she smiles. Many would find such a person repulsive and their instinct would be to turn away. Mother Teresa's response is to see in that disfigured face the face of Jesus. Her work is then not really a human being merely helping another human being. She sees her work as a gift given to God.'

Shapla tends to be highly supportive of all religious traditions believing that they are equally valid paths to God. However, both in classroom discussions and in her written assignments which require her to evaluate and express her own personal opinion she often appears unprepared or fails to understand the point when criticisms are made of religious faith. For example, in a discussion following the 2004 Boxing Day tsunami she seemed unable to grasp the point that such an event might cause people to doubt their faith. Her line of argument tended to be repetitious and insensitive:

'Suffering happens because God is testing us. If God wants to test us that's up to God. Anyway the people who died had probably done something wrong so they deserved to die.'

In an essay about whether war could ever be just she makes only a passing reference to arguments to the contrary and tends to rely on repetition and assertion rather than a defensible line of reasoning: 'All war is wrong. It's just murder, murder, murder! So for that reason no war can be a just war. Some people don't agree with me but I think they are wrong.'

Shapla is showing a high level of ability in *learning about religion* but is not gifted in *learning from religion*. The opposite of this, a pupil showing a very high level of ability in *learning from religion* but who is not at all exceptional in *learning about religion*, may be seen in the following example:

### Case example 6 – Gifted in learning from religion: Harry Year 9

Harry does not have a rigorous knowledge or understanding of the different religious traditions he has studied. He is often forgetful of the specific detail of religious life and practice tending to regard a lot of information about the various religious traditions as being trivial detail and not worth retaining.

During one lesson when he was required to feed back as part of a group what they had learnt about the celebration of the Passover (Pesach) he identified the festival with the Exodus story but did not provide any further explanation of why the festival was of such significance within the Jewish community. He also makes little attempt to retain religious vocabulary. For example, in his feedback to the whole class he said the following:

'The Passover is celebrated to remember when the Jews escaped out of Egypt. They all sit down for a nice meal. The men wear these special hats, which are like flat on their head. They eat a special bread which is unleavened so it's also flat, a bit like a cream cracker.'

However, in discussion Harry has strong opinions and an assured and confident manner. He is highly articulate, and has a wide general knowledge which he is able to deploy in a well-organised argument. For example in a discussion about the existence of God, Harry argued:

'I can see how you don't have to believe in God as the universe could quite possibly have started spontaneously with a big bang some 14 billion years ago. I can see how the sun, moon, stars, planets and solar system all came about without having to believe in God. What I can't believe is that lifeless molecules somehow started to replicate themselves. I can't see how from lifeless matter you can get things which are alive. There must have been a living thing that made life happen and for me the thing that made life happen is God.'

Harry also makes imaginative use of analogies to illustrate his point. For example, in a debate about God and evil in the world he said:

'God is not a cosmic bell-boy for whom we can press a button to get things. God has not lost control. God has given us control because he wants us to learn the value of good and evil. Do you want to be a robot only able to do the right thing? Of course you don't.'

Because pupils do not necessarily show the same level of ability in the two attainment targets, distinguishing between the two is crucial when attempting to identify young people who are gifted in RE. It is equally important to have a good grasp of what making progress in the two attainment targets means.

## Making progress in learning about religion

Progression in *learning about religion* involves three main steps. These are:

1. recall
2. description
3. understanding.

*Step 1: Recall*

Recall is knowledge but essentially it is disconnected, factual knowledge about religion. Pupils show recall when they can name and label things associated with religion. For example, a visit to a place of worship is often used as an occasion for a recall activity. Pupils may be required to name items of furniture in a church often using little more than single words like font, lectern, altar, pulpit.

Recall is very low order religious education; so low, that it is hardly worthy of the name. However, the initial gathering of pieces of data is the start of the process.

*Step 2: Description*

Description is still largely factual knowledge about religion but pupils are now able to connect up their knowledge so that they can give accounts of what they know about religion in ways which are more coherent and sustained than mere recall. Still using the example of a church visit, a description, as opposed to a recall account, might be on the lines of the following: 'On first entering the church you are likely to see a font. This is where baptism takes place. As you walk down the church you will see what looks like a large table covered with a cloth. This is the altar. The altar is used for preparing the bread and wine. To the side of the altar . . .'

Description is more than turning single word recall responses into simple sentences. Description requires connections to be made. So, in the example given, a connection has been made between the font and baptism. A connection has also been made between the altar and the preparing of the bread and wine. There is no indication in the example that the writer has any understanding of what either baptism or the preparing of the bread and wine is really about. This happens when pupils achieve the third step.

*Step 3: Understanding*

The third step pupils make when learning about religion is when they are no longer demonstrating only factual knowledge. Instead pupils are able to make sensible responses if asked about the thoughts, feelings, beliefs or emotions of people who are religious. This is a crucial jump from the external phenomena of religion, those things for example that can be seen, heard, touched, smelt and tasted, to those aspects of religious life which are not externally visible but which go on in the hearts, minds and souls of those who are religiously committed.

## The concept of 'understanding' in RE

The significance of 'understanding' over and above mere description or recall for identifying pupils who are gifted in RE has already been hinted at. However, it is necessary to discuss what exactly is meant by 'understanding' and its significance for identifying pupils gifted in RE in more detail. Within RE, when pupils are described as showing 'understanding', the word may be used in one of three main senses: emotional understanding, cognitive understanding and understanding in the sense that understanding leads to faith commitment.

## Emotional understanding

Emotional understanding is when pupils attempt to explain the emotions and feelings of those who have a religious faith. Pupils are no longer merely describing the external phenomenon of a place of worship, a ritual or a ceremony. They are now able, in a sense, to relate to those of faith who are engaged in a ritual, or some other expression of their faith, and provide a fuller account of the phenomenon by identifying some of the emotions or feelings of the adherent.

A typical example of this can be seen in the following which is to be found on the RE National Curriculum website – www.ncaction.org.uk/subjects/re/index.htm. Following a study of the hajj in Islam pupils are set the following assignment:

### The hajj assignment

Imagine that you are a Muslim and that you have just completed your hajj. Write a letter to a friend explaining what you have done and how you felt.

In response to this assignment, a Year 9 student wrote the following:

'. . . The amount of people there just blew me away and I was amazed because we were all here for the same reason. Following the Ka'bah we listened to the sermons which were very interesting and it really touched me. We then went to run between the mountains of Safa and Marwa. Next we remembered the last sermon of Muhammad and then prayed at Mt Arafat. There were many people there and all praying for family, friends and even people they didn't know, so it makes you think everyone must have been prayed for. This whole experience was totally mind blowing and a once in a lifetime experience. I am so glad I saved up the money to get here.'

Typical of assignments of this nature, the passage contains some factual descriptive material, for example:

'. . . we listened to the sermons . . .'

'. . . we then went to run between the mountains of Safa and Marwa . . .'

'. . . and then prayed at Mt Arafat . . .'

'. . . many people there all praying for family, friends . . .'

The passage also contains attempts to articulate those aspects of the pilgrim's experience which are not merely externally descriptive and cannot be clearly witnessed using our five senses, that is the emotions of a pilgrim undertaking the hajj, for example:

'. . . the amount of people there just blew me away . . .'

'. . . I was amazed . . .'

'. . . This whole experience was totally mind blowing . . .'

'. . . I am so glad I saved up the money to get here . . .'

## A benevolent response to faith

The passage is clearly a step up from a merely descriptive account. It indicates that the pupil is aware that the hajj is a moving, awesome, important and fulfilling experience for the pilgrims who undertake it. The pupil is aware that the experience is deeply valued by the pilgrim and so a respectful tone is maintained throughout.

Often, it is the case that this is all that RE assignments ask of pupils as they seem to indicate that the pupil has a tolerant or a benevolent response to the faith of others. Work of this kind suggests that the pupil is comfortable with diversity and is not threatened by difference. The passage contains reasonably good indicators that the pupil is developing the sort of attitudes that support social cohesion. However, there is little in the passage which indicates that the pupil understands why the hajj might be of such importance for a Muslim, or why it might be a 'totally mind blowing' and fulfilling experience. Understanding, in the sense of knowing why such strong emotions and feelings are being generated, as opposed to simply knowing that they are being generated, may be called 'cognitive understanding'.

## Cognitive understanding

Cognitive understanding takes place when pupils attempt to explain the ideas and beliefs, rather than the emotions and feelings, of those who have a religious faith. However, a pupil is not able only to discuss ideas and beliefs. They are able to explain the particular ideas and beliefs which disclose, or at least come close to disclosing, why a ritual, ceremony, festival or any other aspect of a faith may carry such weight with members of that faith.

We use again the example of the hajj assignment but now the assignment is worded as follows:

### The hajj assignment

Imagine that you are a Muslim and that you have just completed your hajj. Write a letter to a friend explaining what difference, if any, the experience of hajj has made to you.

In response to this assignment a Year 9 student, with cognitive understanding, may write the following:

'. . . The amount of people there of different ages, races and colours made me think that if we try, an overwhelming spirit of true brotherhood can exist between people. It was amazing and it made me realise that there can be a unity and peace between people. Next we remembered the last sermon of Muhammad and then prayed at Mt Arafat. Praying at Mt Arafat was like a reminder of the Day of Judgement. On that day all human souls stand before God, praying for forgiveness in the hope that God will let them enter into paradise. The whole experience made me think that I have not lived my life in a way which has made me worthy of a place in paradise. From now on, I must try and be a better person.'

The emphasis in this passage is now not on claiming that the hajj is a moving and awesome experience. Instead the pupil is making reference to Muslim beliefs about the brotherhood of the Ummah and about the Day of Judgement which disclose why the hajj has such significance for pilgrims. The pupil, for example, points out that on the ninth day of the pilgrimage, when pilgrims spend many hours standing in prayer on Mt Arafat, this day is like a dress rehearsal for Judgement Day. Pilgrims after all are on this day dressed in two pieces of white cloth, their ihram. When they die they will be buried in their ihram and when, as Muslims believe, they will be bodily resurrected on the Day of Judgement they will be resurrected wearing their ihram. They will stand before God surrounded by all the other human souls that have lived and on that day of reckoning they will have to answer to their creator for how they have lived their life. How they will spend the rest of eternity will depend on that judgement.

The pupil brings to their account of the pilgrimage that knowledge of Muslim belief and is able to make use of it to explain why pilgrims find the hajj such a powerful and potentially life-altering experience. Pupils that show 'cognitive understanding' are able to identify the ideas and beliefs which crucially lie behind ritual, ceremonies, actions and other examples of religious life without knowledge of which the fundamental motives of participants remain essentially hidden.

An analogy suggested by Wittgenstein may help us here. Imagine if a chess player was asked, 'Why is the King important in chess?' To be given a descriptive account of what the King can do on the chessboard, for example, the piece can move a single space forward or back, right or left, or diagonally, does not make it clear why the King is important. To be given a series of statements which reflect an emotional understanding of its significance, for example, to be told, 'The King is really very special' or 'The King is the most important piece on the board' or 'The King is so amazing' also fails to make it clear why exactly the King has a high status. It is only if the chess player provides a cognitive understanding of the King by explaining what part the King plays in the winning or losing of the game that all becomes clear. For example, a chess player may answer the question, 'Why is the King important in chess?' by saying: 'If the King is in a position so that it can be taken and nothing can be done to prevent the King from being taken, then the King is "checkmated" and the game is lost.'

These words are disclosure words. When they are understood, suddenly why the King is important in chess becomes clear. It is through such disclosure statements that cognitive understanding is achieved. Young people who are very able in RE do not achieve understanding of religion only in the form of 'emotional understanding' or by showing a 'benevolent response' to faith. Where they excel is particularly in the form of 'cognitive understanding'.

## Faith commitment understanding

The third way in which the word 'understanding' may be used which is particularly relevant to the teaching of RE is in the sense in which understanding leads to the affirmation of faith. Some people believe that when a person truly understands a religion, or an aspect of a religion, then understanding must lead to faith commitment. When 'understanding' of a religion takes place, it is suggested, an individual resonates with that religion and that from this faith results. This may take the form of an individual affirming the faith with which the individual has resonated, or it may result in an individual affirming a faith which previously had been strong but which had become pale or even lost. As long as there is no faith commitment then, in some way or other, this must be due to a lack of understanding. St Augustine expressed the same idea when he wrote, 'Understanding is the reward of faith'.

Given the distinction made in RE today between nurturing religious faith and religious education, the use of the word 'understanding' in this faith commitment sense is not often used. Nevertheless, teachers of RE need to be wary of assuming that a confident, faith statement is evidence of understanding and is therefore also evidence of higher order achievement. If we again use an example based on the hajj, suppose the assignment were worded as follows:

### The hajj assignment

Write a letter to a friend explaining what Muslims do on hajj and what your thoughts are about the pilgrimage.

The response of a Year 9 student may be to write the following:

'. . . Next they remember the last sermon of Muhammad and then pray at Mt Arafat. There are many people there all praying for family, friends and even people they didn't know. It made me think how important prayer is in my life. Praying on my own is important but praying with other people I think is a special and amazing experience. Learning about the hajj made me think about my own religion and just how important my faith is in my life.'

The teacher may conclude that by learning about the hajj the student has gained understanding in the sense that the value Muslims place on prayer has resonated with the student and this has given them the confidence to affirm the value of prayer in their own life.

Valuable though this may be from the point of view of the pupil's personal confidence and their own faith commitment, it would be inappropriate to conclude that this response is evidence of higher order understanding and therefore shows high achievement. To help appreciate the distinction between these three principal ways in which the word 'understanding' may be used in RE the table below provides extracts from the three examples discussed placed in columns so that they can more easily be compared.

| Understanding | Understanding | Understanding |
|---|---|---|
| emotional understanding emotions and feelings | cognitive understanding ideas and beliefs | faith commitment understanding affirmation of faith |
| '. . . The amount of people there just blew me away and I was amazed because we were all here for the same reason. Following the Ka'bah we listened to the sermons which were very interesting and it really touched me. We then went to run between the mountains of Safa and Marwa. Next we remembered the last sermon of Muhammad and then prayed at Mt Arafat. There were many people there and all praying for family, friends and even people they didn't know, so it makes you think everyone must have been prayed for. This whole experience was totally mind blowing and a once in a lifetime experience. I am so glad I saved up the money to get here.' | '. . . The amount of people there of different ages, races and colours made me think that if we try, an overwhelming spirit of true brotherhood can exist between people. It was amazing and it made me realise that there can be a unity and peace between people. Next we remembered the last sermon of Muhammad and then prayed at Mt Arafat. Praying at Mt Arafat was like a reminder of the Day of Judgement. On that day all human souls stand before God, praying for forgiveness in the hope that God will, on the Day of Judgement, let them enter into paradise. The whole experience made me think that I have not lived my life in a way which has made me worthy of a place in paradise. From now on, I must try and be a better person.' | '. . . Next they remember the last sermon of Muhammad and then pray at Mt Arafat. There are many people there all praying for family, friends and even people they didn't know. It made me think how important prayer is in my life. Praying on my own is important but praying with other people I think is a special and amazing experience. Learning about the hajj made me think about my own religion and just how important my faith is in my life.' |

Having discussed the concept of 'understanding' means that we are now in a better position to distinguish between pupils who have breadth of knowledge, sometimes called horizontal knowledge, in the subject, in contrast to pupils who have depth of knowledge, or vertical knowledge in the subject.

## Breadth of knowledge

Pupils with breadth of knowledge in RE may show a lot of knowledge about the different religious traditions. However, much of this knowledge is of a relatively superficial nature. Pupils of this kind may be very familiar with religious vocabulary; for example, they may refer to the Jewish festival of the Passover as the Pesach, and know that the unleavened bread is called matzah, or that the bitter herbs are called maror, and that the middle matzah is broken and is known as the afikoman and is eaten as the 'dessert'. Similarly, pupils may have a detailed knowledge of diversity within and between religious traditions. They may, for example, know that prayer beads in Islam usually have 99 or 33 beads, whereas rosary beads have 59 beads and a crucifix, or that the Mala used in Hinduism has 108 beads. However, despite all of this knowledge the pupil may have very little insight into the nature of religious life or what part religion plays in meeting people's deepest needs or answering their profoundest questions. Their knowledge, which may be substantial, is all primarily descriptive knowledge. Very little of what they know could be called 'cognitive understanding'. As the fifth-century Greek philosopher Heraclitus once put it, 'The learning of many things teaches not understanding.'

## Depth of knowledge

In contrast to pupils with breadth of knowledge, pupils with depth of knowledge have what teachers of RE often call 'insight'. Their understanding, much of which but not exclusively so, is cognitive understanding, and enables them to appreciate the significance religion may play in people's lives. It enables them to understand how religion may motivate, guide and inspire a person's life. Edmund Husserl, one of the pioneers of the phenomenological approach to the study of religion called insight of this kind 'eidetic vision'. Eidetic vision is the ability to grasp the essentials, the driving core or the heart of the matter. For example, a young person with depth of knowledge may or may not be familiar with veneer details about the Passover and that the memory of the Passover has left many Jews today with a horror of slavery. They may recognise that running through the minds of many Jewish people there is a love of freedom and a fearsome sense of pride, independence and an unwillingness to allow themselves to lose their freedom and be shackled by others either physically or mentally. Insight of this sort has a much more profound grasp of what the Passover is really about for Jewish people than knowing about the Hebrew word for unleavened bread or bitter herbs. It is pupils with this form of vertical, depth of knowledge about religion who are gifted in RE.

## Academic disciplines and depth

Young people who demonstrate depth of knowledge and hence are gifted in RE usually do so because they have been taught, or they instinctively make use of, one or more academic disciplines which have for a long period of time been associated with the study of religion. These 'disciplines' are:

- psychology

- sociology

- morality

- theology

- philosophy.

A very able child may provide a response which shows 'depth' or 'insight' using any one of these disciplines. For example, seeking to avoid merely a descriptive account of what Muslims do when they undertake obligatory worship, the Salah, a teacher may set the following task:

## Why is prayer important to Muslims?

Imagine you are a Muslim providing a guided tour around a local mosque. Explain to the visitors why prayer is important to Muslims.

There is of course no single, correct answer to this task. However, that doesn't mean to say that all answers are equally good. Possible answers might include:

'Prayer is important to Muslims because it is in the Qur'an.'

'Prayer is important to Muslims because it is one of the Five Pillars of Islam.'

'Prayer is important to Muslims because it is what the Prophet Muhammad taught.'

These are all technically correct and in a sense acceptable answers. However, they are also weak answers as they do not demonstrate 'depth of knowledge', 'insight' or 'eidetic vision'. None of these answers grasps at the heart of what is really happening and discloses what undertaking Salah really means to Muslims. Examples of responses which show 'depth of knowledge' because they each make use of one of the five main disciplines follow.

## Why is prayer important to Muslims? A psychological answer

Prayer is important to Muslims as it can help us from becoming too puffed up with pride and self-conceit. Humans can easily imagine that they have all the answers to life and forget about God. Prayer reminds us that we must bow and humble ourselves before God and not become conceited as God is so much greater than us.

## Why is prayer important to Muslims? A sociological answer

Prayer is important to Muslims as it can help us feel that we are part of a global community, a brotherhood of believers. As I face towards Makkah in prayer I feel I am one of millions of Muslims all around the world who are also turning towards Makkah in prayer. Being part of something so big makes me feel really sure of my faith.

## Why is prayer important to Muslims? A moral answer

Prayer is important to Muslims as taking time out every few hours to calmly and gently stand, bow and prostrate to God I find helps me get on with people around me. Prayer encourages me to be calm and gentle with people. I don't get angry or irritated. Instead I'm patient with people and don't feel I have to be frantically rushing about, being rude or ignoring people.

## Why is prayer important to Muslims? A theological answer

Prayer is important to Muslims as we believe prayer is a gift from God which provides every Muslim five times a day with a chance to clean their inner self. Five times a day God provides a spiritual stream that runs outside your front door or wherever you are, in the form of prayer. By stepping out of this world, into that spiritual stream, you are cleansed on the inside and can return to the normal world feeling pure and refreshed.

## Why is prayer important to Muslims? A philosophical answer

Prayer is important to Muslims as we believe that prayer will help us on the Day of Judgement. We believe that on that day all of us will have to stand in front of God and answer for how we have lived our lives. Those of us who have used the gift of prayer regularly in life have a better chance of God's mercy and of entering into paradise than those who have shunned God's gift of prayer.

These five academic disciplines are not the only disciplines a gifted pupil may make use of when giving a 'depth' answer. In 1977 the Schools Council published *A Groundplan for the Study of Religion*, in which a similar breakdown of how disciplines like psychology and sociology may contribute to the study of religion was suggested. It also included other disciplines like history and aesthetics.

The key then to identifying high ability in RE is not, 'Do they know a lot about religion?' Much more important is how effective a young person is in making use of disciplines like psychology, sociology and theology to analyse, explain and show an 'insight' into what religion means from the point of view of the adherent. These same disciplines are also important in making progress in *learning from religion*, alongside other skills like reasoning and evaluation. However, this aspect of RE will be explored in the next chapter.

## Summary

- Make use of available data and avoid stereotyping.

- Consciously look out for signs of high ability.

- Being gifted in RE is not the same as being devout, spiritual or socially concerned.

- Pupils are not equally accomplished in *learning about* and *learning from religion*.

- Cognitive understanding is more crucial than description.

- Depth of knowledge or 'insight' requires making use of different academic disciplines.

CHAPTER 4

# Classroom provision

- Classroom organisation and planning
- Poor task setting
- Thinking skills
- Bloom's taxonomy

## Classroom organisation and planning

It is the view of some people that the only way in which very able pupils in RE can be effectively challenged is by the use of bolt-on extras which take place away from the mainstream classroom. Additional activities outside the classroom, for example, special visits, summer schools, after-school clubs and Saturday morning masterclasses, all have their place as part of an RE department's gifted and talented provision. Indeed, this form of beyond the classroom provision is discussed in Chapter 7. However, the main arena for providing for pupils gifted in RE is the RE classroom.

Additional activities, like RE competitions and after-school philosophy clubs, are a valuable bonus. They are not to be sniffed at; nevertheless, they are fringe events to what must be regarded as the main show, the RE lesson. There is little to be gained by providing stimulating activities for very able pupils in an RE club every Tuesday after school, if those same children are bored and treading water, undertaking mundane activities every week as they sit through their RE lesson. An RE department that cannot provide appropriate challenge for very able young people in the classroom, no matter how good its other forms of provision might be, is not providing effective gifted and talented education. The emphasis on the role of the RE classroom as the main instrument for challenging very able young people might alarm some teachers. The fear is that if a teacher ensures that very able children make good or even excellent progress, they can only do so by passing over the heads of the less able, the average or even the able pupils who are in the class. Inevitably this means that pupils other than those who are very able will suffer. The progress of very able pupils, it is suggested, can only be bought at the expense of other pupils.

This is a legitimate concern. However, the truth is that, more often than not, what is good provision for young people gifted in RE is usually also good provision for all children.

## Planning

The goal then is to achieve high quality teaching and learning in RE across the board for all children. That includes high quality teaching and learning for the not so able pupil and also for the exceptionally able pupil. Teachers of RE will find that they are attempting to achieve this in schools in which the general planning arrangements may vary a great deal. Some of this general planning may be part of the school's policy and so is outside of the control of an RE department or of any individual teacher. Nevertheless, a teacher of RE has to work as effectively as possible to deliver quality provision within the system as they find it. To achieve this teachers should be aware of the advantages, but also the possible pitfalls, which may exist in the system they are working within. Other arrangements, such as using teaching assistants and planning activities out of school, will be looked at later but for now we need to consider four types of school planning which have most impact on the classroom. They are:

- mixed ability classes

- setting

- group seating

- extension projects.

### Mixed ability classes

A mixed ability class is one in which the class includes all, or virtually all, of the school's entire ability range. A teacher of RE with a mixed ability class could expect to have pupils who range from being exceptionally able through to some pupils who have very real, or perhaps even severe, learning difficulties. Problematic though this may seem for the effective teaching of very able pupils, mixed ability teaching has at least two main advantages.

The first is that mixed ability teaching has a better chance of avoiding the undoubted demoralising effect which placing pupils into ability sets or streams can have on both pupils and teachers. A young person who is gifted in RE but may be a late developer, or has a specific learning difficulty, may be placed into a lower set. With low expectation a self-fulfilling prophecy takes effect and that young person's gift for RE never blossoms and is never recognised.

The second advantage of mixed ability teaching from the point of view of the teacher of RE is based on the idea that children learn from each other socially, emotionally and culturally. By mixing together young people who may have a very different experience of life outside school, children's thinking and understanding can be informed in ways which otherwise just wouldn't happen. For example, during a Year 9 lesson the class discussed the New Testament teaching, 'Do not return evil for evil' (1 Peter 3:9). During the discussion the effectiveness of prison and whether it was evil to put a person in prison was introduced. A pupil called Ian, who lives with his mother and two brothers and is waiting to be rehoused by the council, spoke up saying: 'Punishing people just makes them worse. What use is prison? It rarely reforms people. My uncle was locked up for stealing to pay for his marijuana habit. When he came out he was addicted to heroin. How did that happen? Not returning evil with evil hasn't failed. It's something that's never seriously been tried.'

As Ian spoke some very able young people had their ideas challenged. They were vividly made aware of an experience of life which it would be highly unlikely they would otherwise have encountered. At the same time Ian suddenly caught the teacher's eye as a pupil who is articulate and skilled at handling ideas and may be much more capable than previously was ever suspected.

A teacher of RE teaching a mixed ability class does, however, need to think very hard about how all of the children in the class can be most effectively taught. This may involve, as in the case of a class discussion, some whole-class teaching but it will also involve some form of differentiation which in a mixed ability class can be a substantial challenge. Planning for the average in the class and letting the less able, or the most able, get by is not an option.

## Setting

Pupils may be taught in subject-specific sets so that the very able pupils are placed in the top sets for RE. This arrangement is quite rare in RE. It is much more likely that pupils will be streamed based on their general ability. Either arrangement may be thought by some to resolve the differentiation issue. However, in reality although the top sets or streams may contain all of the pupils identified as being gifted in RE, that does not eliminate the need to differentiate. Not all of the pupils in the top sets will be very able in RE. Some may be able, or well above average, and lessons will need to be planned to take this into account. It is also quite possible, as can happen with mixed ability teaching, that very able pupils may be placed into lower sets. These will include pupils who are gifted in RE but have not been identified because for one reason or another they are underachieving. It is also very likely that pupils who have the potential to be gifted in RE are placed in lower sets as their potential has not yet been realised.

## Group seating

Pupils often select for themselves where they will sit in a classroom and who they will sit next to. Group seating involves organising all of the pupils in a class on a regular basis into a group of perhaps 4 or 5 pupils. Each group is matched for ability resulting in a very able group, an above average group and so on. This arrangement is thought to be helpful particularly for distributing tasks which are differentiated. For example, a very able group sitting together may be invited to study a difficult text, perhaps an extract from Gandhi's writings on 'satyagraha' and to decide in different circumstances whether his ideas would really work.

Meanwhile a less able group may be asked to look at various resources about Gandhi including a few internet sites and design a home page for their own Gandhi website.

Group seating can be an effective way of ensuring that very able pupils are given challenging tasks, while other pupils are also given tasks which stretch them, but do not result in frustration. On the negative side of course if tasks are not well planned it can have the same 'self-fulfilling prophecy effect' associated with setting. Less able pupils may feel patronised and experience resentment if they are publicly and repeatedly given tasks which are trivial compared to what they see their peers undertaking.

Group seating, rather like setting, does make it overtly clear which pupils are judged to be very able, which are seen as being average, and which pupils are considered less able. Some teachers are offended by the openness of this arrangement and believe it to be divisive and inappropriate particularly for the teaching of less able pupils. Its effectiveness depends much upon the quality of the rapport the teacher has with all members of the class and, of course, on the quality of the differentiated tasks each group is given. In the right hands it is a useful weapon in an RE teacher's arsenal. Some teachers find group seating works best not as a regular arrangement, but as something which is organised from time to time.

## Extension projects

Some teachers of RE plan extension projects in order to provide challenge for very able pupils. This system can be used whether pupils are set for RE or taught in mixed ability classes. It requires pupils to demonstrate independent learning skills by undertaking a project. A time period of perhaps four to six weeks is set aside during which formal weekly homework may be suspended, and even some lesson time may be made available, while pupils undertake their project.

A project may literally be an extension of a classroom topic. For example, a series of lessons on Islam and a visit to a local mosque may result in a child wishing to make a study of mosque design and how it reflects Muslim beliefs. Alternatively, a pupil may wish to break free of anything in the school's RE curriculum and explore something which they personally find rewarding, for example, 'A survey of young people's views on New Age Spirituality'.

An extension project can be a very rewarding undertaking. Being given the opportunity to have a much freer rein is a liberating experience for some pupils and can result in pupils committing vast quantities of energy and time leading to work which is of staggering quality and maturity. Other advantages include:

- helps develop independent learning skills

- gives pupils an opportunity to express themselves at length

- develops specialist knowledge in depth

- taps into a pupil's natural wish to pursue areas which interest them

- models the adult world helping pupils to become pioneers in a field of study.

However, as with 'group learning', extension projects should be seen as just one of the weapons which a teacher of RE might use. Extension projects often motivate pupils because they have a certain novelty appeal. A continuous round of 'extension projects' would soon lose effectiveness and would be unlikely to provide a coherent programme of religious education. Even if extension projects are used only sparingly the following drawbacks are important to bear in mind:

- not all very able pupils are self-motivated or keen to learn

- pupils may well need a substantial amount of monitoring and in some cases support, all of which can be very time consuming

- while some pupils may find working on a extension project rewarding, others may find such a task beyond them and need the structure of more formal teaching

- criteria for what makes for a good project have to be made clear to pupils as some pupils do not always properly understand what is expected of them in an extension project. They may produce a project which is little more than plagiarised copying and is very weak in terms of analysis, explanation, reasoning or evaluation.

## Poor task setting

A teacher of RE may have to work in a prescribed system which they cannot do much about. However, many of the day-to-day classroom tasks pupils are asked to undertake are usually directly in the hands of the teacher. An important step in providing a challenging learning environment for very able pupils, and one which is also important for providing high quality teaching and learning across the board, is the elimination of poor tasks.

RE is prone to poor task setting. Poor tasks in RE are those tasks which are of dubious educational value. They tend to concentrate on lower order skills, like naming, identifying and recall. RE is frequently seen as being a contentious area and so 'keeping to the facts' and using predictable tasks tends to be regarded as a safe option. However, the result is often that such tasks do little more than keep children busy. They give the illusion of children making progress whereas in reality very little useful learning is taking place.

This is not just a problem teachers of RE are prone to. Commercially available RE books are not always exemplars of good practice. It is not unknown for RE textbooks to have accurate information and excellent visual material but have a list of suggested activities and tasks some of which are of doubtful value. However, we mustn't be too critical of textbooks or of classroom practice. RE has spent many years trying to resolve issues over content and not enough thought has been given to the business of classroom practice. Also our knowledge of how young people learn has moved on substantially over the last ten years or so. Few of us could say that tasks we set in an RE classroom a decade ago have worn well and are just as valid today. Teachers of RE need to develop their critical skills and learn to recognise those tasks which are effective and valuable, and weed out those tasks that pupils can undertake by engaging little more than second gear.

Consider the following examples:

- **copying**. Pupils are asked to copy out passages of text, particularly translated passages of sacred text. This is to a degree based on the belief that some passages are crucial, 'must know' pieces of information and that copying helps achieve this. Pupils are also invited to copy out passages duplicating scripts which they do not understand like Sanskrit, Arabic or Hebrew. By doing so this mimics the actions of devotees and somehow helps pupils become more appreciative of the text and aware of the mind and feelings of the adherent.

- **drawing**. Pupils are invited to draw an object associated with a religion, for example, a religious artefact, a symbol, a person in a prayer position, a religious shrine or an item of religious furniture. This is seen as a way of helping pupils become familiar with such objects and aids learning. However, it is questionable whether time spent looking at an object while drawing it results in a very strong memory of that object, unless the pupil is making a conscious effort to commit the image to memory. It is also questionable as to the value of spending time focused on an object's appearance when the real consideration is what does it mean, or signify, or tell us about faith.

- **clozed tasks**. Pupils are given a text containing missing words. The missing words are usually randomly chosen and pupils are invited to write in the missing words in the spaces left vacant. However, the mental energy of most children is often on completing the task. This may be achieved by skim reading and using signals like grammatical structure to identify the missing words rather than attempting to understand the sense of the text itself. It may be doubted whether much understanding of the text takes place, or if pupils commit much in the way of the ideas, words or information in the text to memory.

- **wordsearch**. Hidden in a maze of letters are some key religious words. Pupils are asked to highlight those words. By doing so pupils are thought to be more likely to become familiar with those words and make use of them in the future. The emphasis of the task is on spotting the word in among distracters. Pupils are not being asked to practise the skill of using the words correctly in context. It is not at all clear that being able to recognise a word in amongst others will help a pupil to make correct use of that word in the future.

- **recall questions**. Pupils are given text to read after which they are asked to answer a series of questions. The answers to the questions may be found by revisiting the text and using the words in the text to answer the questions. Most pupils tend to focus on answering the question rather than undertaking a careful reading of the passage. Pupils skim read the text looking for the answers. This is sometimes claimed to be a 'comprehension' exercise testing pupils' ability to understand the text. However, this is rarely the case. Often the task is little more than, as Barbara Wintersgill has described it, a 'retrieval of information from a page of textbook or worksheet'. Pupils are not usually asked and are not likely to commit their answers to either medium or long term memory. Questions tend not to be discursive but are limited to questions of fact and so often focus on peripheral features of a religion and can be answered with a single word, a fragment of a sentence or a single sentence, for example, 'What are the other names for Durga?' 'What title do Jews give Abraham?'

- **discipline drift**. After being taught about an aspect of a religion pupils are set a question which has only tenuous links with religion or the original subject matter. The task itself may be quite challenging, requiring some research skills or thoughtful consideration. However, challenge has only been achieved by drifting into general knowledge or another discipline and does not contribute to the aims of religious education. For example, after learning about the oral tradition associated with Hindu scripture, pupils are asked, 'How important should memory training be today?' Following an account of a religious naming ceremony pupils are asked to, 'Find out what your name means and why you were given it'.

- **labelled diagram**. Pupils are asked to draw or often copy a diagram and label the main features. A typical task might state, 'Draw your own diagram to show the Five Pillars of Islam. Label each of the pillars to explain what they are' or 'Draw a Seder plate and label the items on the plate. Explain what each of the items symbolise.' Often the information is provided either in the form of an actual diagram or else is directly referred to in the text. Although words like 'explain' may be used to describe the task, in reality the task is little more than a copying activity which involves transferring information from a text format into a diagrammatic format.

- **signally low expectations**. Poor task setting can sometimes be seen not so much in the task itself but in signals that a teacher may give that only shallow or obvious answers are expected. Such signals may be in the form of allowing limited time for a response or by providing very restricted space for an answer. The task itself might offer challenge but in reality little more than a short recall response is the signalled expectation. For example, pupils might be asked, 'What does Christmas celebrate?' Potentially the task could be a challenging one. Pupils may explain that Christmas celebrates the incarnation of God on earth, that it marks a unique moment in the history of the salvation of humankind. Or they may suggest that Christmas celebrates the belief that peace and goodwill can exist between all humankind. However, the question may be only one of several questions all of which are to be completed in five minutes. Or perhaps, following the question, a single line is provided suggesting that only a brief answer is expected. In such circumstances pupils learn that the simple, recall answer – 'Christmas celebrates the birth of Jesus' is all that is required. Such an answer could have been provided by a pupil in Year 2, and yet it is known that the same level of response remains acceptable in some Key Stage 3 classrooms.

- **design tasks**. Pupils are asked to design and often make an object which is associated with a religion. For example, 'Design and make a Christmas card', 'Make your own Divali diva lamp', 'Design a Muslim prayer mat'. The word 'design' suggests a problem-solving activity, which requires the student to show originality while working within certain challenging parameters. However, often the task is presented with no parameters, or only very vague ones. Hardly anything is provided in the way of RE criteria. In such cases any finished outcome is seen as being successful. So, for example, a Christmas card design may be seen as being equally successful whether it is decorated with sprigs of holly, snowmen, Christmas trees or three wise men. A Muslim prayer mat design may be judged to be equally appropriate as long as abstract patterns are used, whether the abstract patterns in the design are geometric, asymmetric, floral or based on little more than a wavy line.

- **opinion tasks**. A similar apparent willingness to accept 'any answer as good' can be seen in tasks which invite pupils to express their opinion or state what they think, but they are not required to justify, give reasons or identify evidence to support their view. For example, during a lesson on religious rules pupils are invited to suggest, 'What new school rule would you bring in?' Or during a lesson on eternal life pupils are asked, 'What do you think happens after death?' Such tasks may be seen as being good opportunities for pupils to be thoughtful, creative and imaginative. However, without being asked to support their answers with any form of evidence or justification pupils can engage in little more than fanciful or indulgent speculation. For example, pupils may suggest that a good new school rule would be to 'install chocolate fountains in every classroom' or after death you have another life where 'boys are good looking and aren't naff'.

Identifying and weeding out poor tasks is a necessary step towards ensuring that very able pupils are challenged in RE. However, clearing out poor tasks is really the easy part. Replacing poor tasks with much better tasks which have a high educational value is much more difficult. There is, however, a substantial body of work which can be of direct help to the teacher of RE. This is to be found in a collection of classroom activities and ideas which are associated with the development of what is usually called 'thinking skills'.

## Thinking skills

Through the work of people like Carol McGuiness at Queen's University, Belfast and the Thinking Skills Research Centre at the University of Newcastle there has emerged a number of classroom tasks which do challenge pupils and are very suited to the teaching of RE. Vivienne Baumfield in her important book *Thinking through Religious Education* (2002) provides a rationale, examples and also specific teaching advice on classroom tasks. These tasks avoid routine activities like description, recall, labelling and drawing which are all too often the staple diet of RE. Instead 'thinking skills' activities have the following characteristics:

- open-ended with multiple solutions

- encourage pupils to evaluate or make judgements

- require pupils to give reasons and to justify their judgements

- pose problem-solving activities which have a realistic context

- require pupils to analyse knowledge and apply it or put it to use.

Vivienne Baumfield provides RE examples of nine 'thinking skills' activities. They are:

- odd one out

- classification

- fact or opinion

- fortune lines

- map from memory

- reading images

- mysteries

- story telling

- community of enquiry.

Many of these activities are increasingly being adopted by teachers of RE. Often the claim is made that they not only successfully challenge very able pupils but that they can also be used as whole-class activities, even where classes are mixed ability. In other words, they generally raise the level of challenge to the benefit of all pupils.

To give a flavour of how these activities raise the level of challenge in RE, four particularly useful activities, odd one out, mysteries, community of enquiry and reading images, are described.

## Odd one out

Odd one out usually involves pupils working in pairs, or in groups of three or four, to consider three objects, places or people and decide which of the three is the odd one out. Baumfield provides two examples of this strategy. One is based on Jewish artefacts and the other relates to the structure of the Roman Catholic Church, for example:

---

**Example 1 – Jewish artefacts**

tefillin          mezuzah       kippah

Which is the odd one out and why?

**Example 2 – The Roman Catholic Church**

the Pope          priests          bishops

Which is the odd one out and why?

---

Odd one out as a strategy involves making it clear that:

- there is not necessarily a right or wrong answer

- pupils must give a reason, or reasons, to support their answer and it is the quality of their reasoning which is crucial.

The strategy avoids the mere transmission of information which requires pupils to be passive recipients of information from the teacher. The emphasis is upon the pupils, not the teacher, to do the work. They have to work together to pool what information they have, or can gain, about the choices available and then analyse that information looking for similarities and differences.

Teachers that use this strategy are often surprised that the pupils know a lot already about the choices they are being asked to consider. This may be due to general knowledge which very able pupils just pick up. Or it may be due to learning in RE which took place in Key Stage 2 which the secondary teacher of RE is completely unaware of. It is often suspected that many very able pupils in Key Stage 3 are mildly bored in their RE lessons as they revisit material which they previously learnt about and understood well in Key Stage 2.

Odd one out as an activity for the RE classroom doesn't have to be limited to explicit religious material. Pupils can show a remarkable grasp of subtle distinctions if they are asked to consider the differences between the secular and the sacred or between religious concepts. For example, which of the following is the odd one out?

a pilgrim          a holidaymaker          a tourist

## Mysteries

Mysteries, as the name implies, involves the pupils in detective work about a key question, the answer to which is not at all clear cut. Baumfield gives two examples of mysteries. One is about a Jewish boy approaching the age of thirteen and the key question the pupils have to answer is, 'Why is Simon going to Jerusalem?' The other example is about a seventeen-year-old girl who is a committed Christian and the key question is, 'Will Fiona have an abortion?'

To help the pupils to solve the problem they are usually asked to work in groups of three or four. Each group is given 16–30 pieces of information. Each piece of information is normally brief and printed onto individual pieces of paper. Some of this information may be very relevant and suggest one answer. Some information may be equally relevant but suggest a completely different answer or answers. Some of the information may look relevant but may in fact be a red herring. Pupils are given usually around thirty minutes to discuss the information.

### A mysteries example – should Mr and Mrs Robinson have their baby baptised?

Four months ago Linda Robinson gave birth to their first baby. Both Linda and her husband Dave Robinson are thinking of having the baby baptised. Should they?

| | |
|---|---|
| All of Linda's brothers and sisters have been baptised. In Linda's family baptism is a tradition which everyone enjoys. | Simon, a friend of Dave, says you can be a Christian but not be baptised or go to church. |
| Jesus was baptised when he was about 30 years old. | Most Sundays Dave plays football for a local Sunday league team. |
| Linda believes that baptism is a way of saying thank you to God for being given a baby. | As well as baptism most Anglican churches require confirmation which takes place when the person is old enough to decide for themselves. |
| A member of the church which Linda goes to says that the Church has gone soft and allows people to make vows which they don't really believe in. | Dave says he believes in God but the last time he was inside a church was four years ago when he was married. |
| For over a thousand years the custom in many Christian churches has been to baptise infants, quite soon after they are born. | When a baby is baptised the godparents have to say that they believe in Christ and that they renounce evil. |
| The priest in Linda's church says that baptism is the first step to becoming a member of the Church. | Dave says that there must be some sort of God that started the world but he doesn't really believe in the Trinity or that Jesus is the Son of God. |
| A person can be baptised at any age. If a person wasn't baptised as a baby they can decide for themselves as an adult if they want to be baptised. | Linda's father says that only a baptised baby can be a child of God and can enter the Kingdom of Heaven. |
| During baptism water is poured onto the child's head as a sign of becoming a member of the Church in a clean and pure state. | The local priest has said to Linda that it would be nice to see Dave in church and that he hopes he will have a chance to baptise her baby. |

| | |
|---|---|
| A member of Linda's church tells her that baptism may mean many things. It may mean celebrating the baby's birth or it may be about being made a child of God. Only God knows. | For over three hundred years after Jesus died most Christians were baptised only when they were adults. |
| Dave says that a baby should be allowed to grow up and then when they are older they can make up their own mind if they want to be baptised. | Linda's mother says that she loves baptisms as 'they are a great family get-together.' |
| Linda regularly goes to her local parish church. When asked about her religion she says she is 'Church of England'. | During baptism, the priest pours a little of the water onto the child's head and says, 'I baptise you in the name of the Father, and of the Son, and of the Holy Spirit.' |
| Friends of Dave and Linda tell them that their baptism was 'Great. It was like telling the whole world that we wanted our baby to be part of God's family.' | Linda's sister says that she would really like to be her baby's godmother as she thinks babies are adorable. |

To solve the mystery pupils find that they have to:

- become familiar with the various pieces of information

- evaluate the information's relevance and weigh up its worth

- classify the information, deciding on whether it supports a possible solution

- communicate and agree on a persuasive argument to justify the answer they finally arrive at.

The strategy does depend on pupils, or at least some of the pupils in each group, having reading skills. However, as this information is provided in small packages it is a great deal less daunting than a page of text. The experience of most teachers is that it can be used with classes which are mixed ability and that it stimulates a great deal of discussion amongst pupils. Above all the strategy provides an excellent opportunity for pupils not to simply manipulate bits of information on paper around a table but to articulate ideas, rehearse arguments, speculate using available evidence and to practise making a reasoned judgement. As speaking is a precursor to writing, the strategy can directly raise the quality of all pupils' extended writing in RE including the writing of the most able.

## Community of enquiry

Community of enquiry involves consciously changing the direction of the flow of ideas and information in a classroom. The teacher of RE holds back and does not take centre stage in the classroom. They are no longer the primary transmitter of information, or the person in the classroom who raises the questions or sets the agenda. Instead it is the pupils who get to raise their questions, it is the pupils who mainly decide the direction the lesson will take and it is the pupils that do most of the talking. The emphasis is on the quality of pupils' learning not on the virtuosity of the teacher's performance. The pupils are now no longer perceived as youngsters who don't know and so have to be taught. Instead they become a community of learners that are engaged in their enquiry, and as a community they will largely be responsible for the direction the enquiry will take.

The source of many of these ideas was Matthew Lipman. As a professor of philosophy at Columbia University in the late 1960s Lipman was appalled at the inability, which many young people seemed to show, to be able to use reason and to be able to think for themselves. In an attempt to encourage young people to become 'more thoughtful, more reflective, more considerate and more reasonable individuals' he advocated a 'community of enquiry'. In a community of enquiry young people were to engage in dialogue as a cooperative venture. Today community of enquiry forms a central plank in the 'Philosophy for Children' movement of which Lipman is a pioneer.

### Learning through talking

Central to Lipman's ideas is the belief that we learn by talking. We do not really learn to think by only listening to other people, like teachers expressing their thoughts out loud in front of us. In the same way, our ability to play tennis doesn't really improve much by sitting in a chair watching Wimbledon for a fortnight. To get good at thinking we have to talk with others, formulate our arguments in public and practise articulating our views out loud. Even when we walk away from a discussion a common experience is that our brain continues to race, thinking over what we said and how we could have put it better. Following a discussion we think about what others had said and how we might have agreed with or countered their arguments. Discussion isn't something which happens as a culmination of learning. Discussion shouldn't be something pupils are only allowed to do after they have carefully been taught about 'the issue' exploring the viewpoints of lots of other people. Discussion is what fires up and motivates young people to want to think and learn. Even though their discussion and their argument might be flawed and not as well informed as we might like, to defer discussion until such a point that we feel they are ready and 'can do it properly' is likely only to dampen the flames or, worse, extinguish the spark.

Discussion in which there is a vibrant exchange of ideas should therefore be a regular feature of challenging RE. However, often what passes for discussion in the RE classroom is a stilted affair with limited contributions from pupils. Most of these contributions are directed towards the teacher. The teacher provides a sort of commentary, 'So, Haleemah, you think holy books are still relevant today. Who would like to support Haleemah's view?' Or perhaps rather lamely the teacher attempts to keep the discussion going, 'That's an interesting idea, Emily. Is there anybody who has a different view?' Genuine reciprocal discussion, in which there is repeated pupil to pupil interaction, a ding-dong of ideas in which the teacher plays no obvious part, is quite rare. This is where community of enquiry comes in. It provides a strategy under which reciprocal discussion is much more likely to flourish.

## How does community of enquiry work?

Community of enquiry involves some sort of initial stimulus. This may be an image, an object, a religious artefact, a video clip, a story or perhaps a newspaper cutting. Instead of inviting pupils to respond to a series of questions which originate from the teacher, pupils are asked to reflect on the stimulus and think of the question which the stimulus raises in their minds and which they think the class should discuss.

Images are particularly potent when used with young people today. They readily respond to all sorts of images, forming poignant and direct questions which teachers sometimes only tentatively elude to, believing them to be too hard, sensitive or provocative. Images may be overtly religious but they do not have to be. For example, a Renaissance artist's image of Jesus healing a blind man may raise the question 'Are the miracles of Jesus really true?' An image showing a mushroom cloud following a nuclear explosion may give rise to the question 'Will humans one day destroy themselves?'

### Reflection time

Pupils shouldn't be rushed into coming up with their question. To achieve thinking classrooms, thinking time must be provided. Pupils may be invited to study the stimulus in silence for perhaps a minute and then are given a further two minutes to come up with their question.

### Snowballing

Pupils may then be invited to share their question with a partner and agree amongst the two of them which question they like most. Pairs of pupils may then double up into groups of four and as a group of four decide which question is most interesting. By this stage any flippant or frivolous questions are usually weeded out. Often what emerges are slightly maverick questions which appeal to young people but are still nevertheless very appropriate RE questions.

### Democratic vote

A class of thirty or so young people might be expected to generate eight or more questions for discussion. All eight questions are posted up for the whole class to see and the class decides based on a democratic vote, or series of votes, which of the eight questions the class will discuss.

Once the class itself has decided the question to be discussed, the discussion itself is greatly aided by additional ideas which are part of the community of enquiry strategy. These are outlined below.

### Seating

The seating dynamics of the classroom have a profound effect on whether reciprocal discussion really takes place or not. Discussion is notoriously difficult if pupils are sitting in groups or worse still in rows. The dynamics of the classroom are such that nearly all contributions from the pupils are inevitably directed at the teacher who stands at the focal point of the classroom. Time spent changing the classroom dynamics so that everybody is sitting in a large circle or perhaps a horseshoe is time well spent. Either a circle or a horseshoe enables participants to be able to see each other and gives each person more or less equal status in the classroom.

### Listening response

Before the discussion begins pupils are reminded of the importance of listening to what other pupils say. Sometimes it is suggested that all pupils are required to begin any contribution they make to the discussion with the words, *'I agree/disagree with . . . because . . .'* However, this can often make the discussion a little formal. Alternatively, the teacher may ask for a volunteer to report back after the discussion is over on how well they thought contributors responded to what other people had to say. Even if no one volunteers pupils are often sufficiently alerted to making a listening response that they tend to do so anyway.

### Encouraging broad participation

Frequently class discussions are dominated by a few individuals. These are not necessarily the most able pupils but tend to be the most competitive or opinionated. The shift in seating arrangements can help encourage wider participation but an additional strategy can be to make use of speech cards. Each pupil is given four speech cards. Every time a pupil makes a contribution to the discussion they have to sacrifice a speech card. Once they have used up all their speech cards they can make no further contribution to the discussion. This has the effect of discouraging pupils from making jokey or thoughtless asides thereby wasting speech cards. It also encourages pupils that may be very able but reluctant to speak to join in the discussion as they feel obliged to use up at least some of their speech cards.

### The role of the teacher

Using community of enquiry, the role of the teacher is not to contribute to the discussion but to be an interested and active listener. Before the discussion begins the teacher should make it clear that they themselves will not be joining in. They will be listening and are very interested in what people have to say. Some teachers find this very hard and feel that there are times in a discussion when they have to say something, perhaps to direct the discussion in a particular direction or to correct something that has been said. This is always a mistake. For some pupils once they are aware that it is possible that the teacher may join in they clam up and never speak. For example, on one occasion a pupil said something in a discussion only to find this followed by a 'correction' from the teacher. This made the pupil feel so uncomfortable that they didn't speak again in an RE lesson for two years. Also once pupils become aware that the teacher will join in, they become less motivated to actually instigate the discussion themselves. They learn that they can always sit back and wait and sooner or later the teacher will become impatient and will say something in an attempt to get the discussion started. Often teachers that are the most successful exponents of community of enquiry deliberately adopt a head-down but listening body language. They avoid eye contact with the pupils as this again can put pupils off and can make them reluctant to join in.

### The language of respect

In order to try and encourage exchanges between pupils that are courteous and not too adversarial some teachers negotiate 'ground rules' with pupils, such as not interrupting someone who is speaking, no abusive language, not raising the voice or always using the language of respect.

## Reading images

The potency images have for young people and how they can be used to stimulate questions for discussion has already been referred to. However, often in RE images are used only as an illustration. More adventurously they are sometimes used as a source from which pupils can gain information. This activity is usually called 'the 5Ws'. This involves asking pupils to gather information from a picture, or pictures, for example, of Hindus celebrating Divali or perhaps of a scene showing a baptism. Pupils are asked to study the picture carefully and extract from the picture all the information they can by asking 'Who?', 'What?', 'Where?', 'When?' and 'Why?'

However, the first four of these questions almost invariably results in little more than description or recall. It is true that pupils are being required to mentally work harder to extract information from the picture than they would if they were simply told. Nevertheless, it is questionable whether the strategy really makes very substantial demands upon very able pupils.

The fifth, 'Why?', question is a challenging one but often it is only summarily undertaken or even neglected while pupils use up valuable time responding to the other 'W' questions. The human mind, like water, often follows the line of least resistance. Even very able pupils will not necessarily spend a lot of energy tackling a 'Why?' question when a great portion of time can legitimately be used up on much simpler 'What?' and 'Where?' tasks.

To increase the level of challenge, pupils may be invited not to spend time on the 'Who?' 'What?' 'Where?' and 'When?' tasks but to go straight to the 'Why?' activity. Pupils may be invited to consider particular people in an image and suggest what their thoughts or feelings might be. This requires pupils not spending time on noting those aspects of an image which are physically obvious. Instead pupils have to think about character, attitude, beliefs and relationships.

For example, in Carl Bloch's painting of Peter's denial, Bloch creates an image where at the moment Peter denies Jesus for the third time, Jesus is to be seen in the background being led away by guards. Bloch imagines Jesus is turning back and looks at Peter. A challenging question for pupils to respond to would be, 'What do you think Jesus is thinking at this moment?'

Some pupils may suggest that Jesus is feeling let down by his best friend, or that he is angry. Others may suggest that Jesus is too concerned about himself and what will happen to him to have any thoughts at all about Peter. Very able pupils who have a more subtle grasp of Jesus' character and teaching may recognise Jesus is a man acutely aware of human failings and so is reluctant to find fault in others. As a man who lives by a code of love and forgiveness, Jesus might be looking back at Peter and recognising that he is racked with guilt at having let down his friend. Jesus is filled with compassion and perhaps is trying to communicate to Peter that despite his friend's failure at this moment of trial their relationship is not broken and that the bonds of friendship are still strong.

An additional activity might be to imagine that Peter kept a diary and ask, 'What might Peter write in his diary a few hours later?' Alternatively, pupils might be asked to suggest, 'What might Peter have said about this moment a year later?' Very able pupils might be able to demonstrate their understanding of early Christianity by suggesting 'A year later Peter would have been convinced that although he had shamefully denied him, Jesus had suffered and died, and yet God had resurrected him in glory. All that had happened had been necessary and even Peter's denial had been prophesied. Peter now felt himself to be a very different man from the one he was a year ago. He was now full of courage and determination. He was filled with the Holy Spirit. He felt driven to spread the good news that God is a forgiving God who knows all about human failings and that we need not fear death as eternal life awaits those who have faith in Christ.'

## Contrasting images

As well as using images, pupils may be invited to view two contrasting images. The two images may represent the same scene or very similar scenes but do so in a very different way. In the case of religious art, the two artists may have different views or interpretations and this is reflected in the images they paint. Barbara Wintersgill, for example, in her book *Ways of Saying* (1994) discusses two images which represent Jesus' Transfiguration. One is by Giovanni Bellini and the other is by Sanzio Raphael. Pupils may be invited to study the two images and suggest why they are different. Wintersgill suggests that Bellini tried to produce an image of what really happened. It is an 'historical representation'. Raphael on the other hand tried to produce an image which mainly inspires belief. It is a 'devotional representation'.

The significance of activities of this kind is that they are open to more than one answer. Pupils are not being required merely to learn and regurgitate the facts. They are being required to draw upon what knowledge and ideas they have and to exercise their imagination to come up with a view of their own which isn't just fanciful speculation but is based on a reasonable and balanced judgement.

As well as the view which Barbara Wintersgill suggests, a pupil might argue that Bellini has attempted to produce an image which represents Christ as a man of peace and calm, serenity and tranquillity and yet as a man he remains grounded in this life. Raphael on the other hand sees Christ as a man who is full of dynamic energy and power. As both God and man he is lifted up out of the sordid turmoil of our existence and for a moment we see him bathed in brilliance as Lord and Master, the Son of God.

## Bloom's taxonomy

One of the clearest features of all these 'thinking skills' activities is that they tend to concentrate on the higher end of Benjamin Bloom's well-known taxonomy of cognitive goals. In particular the more challenging activities we have looked at require pupils to evaluate, apply, analyse and, in some cases, synthesise knowledge, ideas and beliefs.

Bloom's taxonomy is usually represented in the form of a pyramid. The pyramid contains six cognitive goals with knowledge – remembering and retaining – always placed at the base of the pyramid as the least demanding of 'cognitive goals'. Evaluation – judging and assessing – is always placed at the top of the pyramid as the most demanding of 'cognitive goals'.

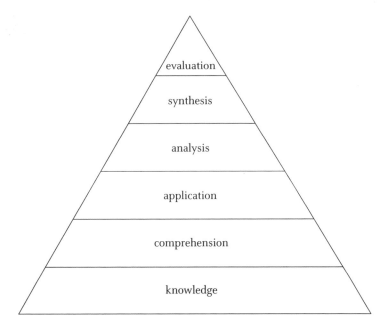

Bloom's taxonomy

To explain more fully what each of the six categories is about, Robert Fisher in *Teaching Children to Think* (1990) provides an illustration using the story of Goldilocks and the Three Bears. Similarly it is possible to see how questioning in RE can vary from the relatively undemanding knowledge level, through to the higher level of difficulty, evaluation, by using the story of the Good Samaritan.

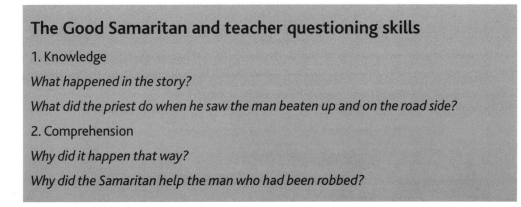

### The Good Samaritan and teacher questioning skills

1. Knowledge

*What happened in the story?*

*What did the priest do when he saw the man beaten up and on the road side?*

2. Comprehension

*Why did it happen that way?*

*Why did the Samaritan help the man who had been robbed?*

3. Application

*What would you have done?*

*What would you do if you saw a man who had been beaten up and left on the road side?*

4. Analysis

*Which part did you like best?*

*Which person in the story did you like most?*

5. Synthesis

*Can you think of a different ending?*

*In what other way might the Samaritan have behaved?*

6. Evaluation

*What did you think of the story?*

*Was the priest or the Samaritan right or wrong to do what they did? Why?*

In Bloom's taxonomy it is possible to see what higher order questioning looks like in RE. However, the subject of questioning skills in RE is looked at in more detail in the next chapter.

## Summary

- The classroom is the main arena for challenging the very able.
- Avoid activities which require recall or description.
- Make use of strategies which require evaluation, reasoning, explanation, problem solving, analysis.
- Make use of Bloom's taxonomy and higher order questioning.

CHAPTER 5

# More classroom provision

- Questioning skills
- Alternatives to writing – formal debate
- Changes in the field of study
- Philosophy of religion

## Questioning skills

Questioning plays a very important role in enabling all pupils, including the very able, to make good progress in RE. Some teachers of RE have a natural flair for spontaneously inventing good questions in the classroom. However, most of us have to plan carefully the questions we intend to use. Without prior thought to both main questions and supplementary questions, most teachers tend to fall back on questions which are poorly formed or which only secure knowledge rather than gain understanding or develop thinking. What makes for good questioning in RE?

### A guide to good questioning in RE

- Ask questions of substance which require pupils to show understanding or provide an explanation, or make a judgement, or offer an interpretation or provide a solution to a problem.

- Avoid peripheral questions or questions which only ask for factual recall or description.

- Avoid asking two or three questions together which may confuse pupils – use a single question if possible.

- Be patient and allow pupils thinking time to consider answers.

- Ask pupils to give their reasons to support their judgements.

- Listen accurately to pupils' responses and use what pupils say to form supplementary questions.

- Make use of open questions for which there might be a number of appropriate responses and not just a 'Yes' or 'No' answer.

- Provide a mix of questions some of which are asked of named pupils but some of which are thrown open to the whole class.

- Attempt to clarify a pupil's response by repeating questions in a modified form or by asking the same question sometimes in a positive form, sometimes in its negative form.

- Be persistent, don't give up on a difficult question because the pupils at first appear unwilling to engage.

- Pursue diversity and original thinking by directing questions at pupils if they show views which divert from the norm or show particular awareness.

- Ask questions which call for specific examples to avoid vague abstractions or platitudinous generalisations.

- Use supplementary questions to probe pupils' responses which are unclear or evasive.

- Try to use other pupils in the class to correct inaccurate answers or false information rather than simply telling pupils answers or publicly correcting them.

- Raise questions which are 'in the news' or have a contemporary relevance.

- Avoid questions which really only concern members of organised religion and are unlikely to be of much relevance to young people.

## Using questioning to lead a discussion

The following classroom exchange gives examples of how many of the suggestions in the 'guide to good questioning' may be put into practice.

1. Teacher      What do you think of the work of Christian Aid which helps the very poor in the world? Is that work we should all be supporting?

The teacher avoids a factual recall question like 'How is money raised in Christian Aid week?' or 'Can you name some countries in which Christian Aid works?'

Factual recall questions might guarantee a response from pupils but they are peripheral to much more difficult but important questions like the impact religion has on people's lives, or whether wealthy nations have a duty to help poorer nations, or whether aid agencies are really effective.

However, the teacher has asked two questions. The first is an open question to which a single 'Yes' or 'No' response would not make sense. This is followed by a closed question to which the response may be little more than 'Yes' or 'No'.

2. Natalie      Yes

Natalie provides a compliant and what some might see as a safe answer. The conventional view is that the work of aid agencies like Christian Aid should be supported. To give a 'No' response is a much more controversial position.

However, Natalie doesn't elaborate on what she has said. She ignores the teacher's first open question and responds only to the teacher's second closed question.

There is no general murmur of consent from the rest of the class.

3. Teacher     Who thinks that we shouldn't support the work of Christian Aid? (No one responds)

The teacher repeats the original closed question (1) but this time in its negative form. The lack of response from the pupils may be due to the understandable unwillingness of young people to stand out from their peers by expressing their views in public. Also the lack of response may be due to the fact that unless an issue raises very strong views most people are reluctant to support a negative view.

As the pupils appear unwilling to engage in a discussion the temptation is to break off at this point and revert to more straightforward recall questions which do illicit a response. However the teacher is more persistent.

4. Teacher     Who thinks that doing something to help the very poor in the world is a good thing?

The teacher, refusing to be put off by the lack of response from the pupils, restates the original question again (1) but makes an important modification. Instead of asking, 'Is that work we should all be supporting?' which puts pupils on the spot suggesting are they prepared to make a personal commitment, the teacher puts the question more in the form of, 'In principle, is helping the very poor in the world a good thing?'

(All the children except Leon and Kelly put their hands up.)

5. Teacher     Does that mean, Kelly, that you think helping the poor in the world is not a good thing?

Twenty-seven of the twenty-nine pupils in the class support the conventional view. The teacher directs a specific question at one of the two pupils who didn't affirm this conventional view.

Pursuing diversity in the classroom is important and can be fruitful. The teacher checks to see if Kelly really is disagreeing with most of the class by repeating the question (4) but this time in its negative form.

6. Kelly       Sometimes it is good but sometimes it isn't.

Probing Kelly's thinking by the use of the negative question has worked to a degree. Kelly's response indicates that she doesn't hold a clear black and white view that helping the poor is always good.

However, she is reluctant to be drawn and her answer is not grounded with a concrete example. RE discussions at this point often become little more than a series of vague abstractions or peter out in 'airy-fairy' generalisations, e.g. 'Some religions believe this but some religions don't.'

7. Teacher    Why sometimes is it not good to help the poor?

The teacher attempts to clarify Kelly's previous ambivalent answer by trying to probe into what she is saying.

The teacher's question focuses on only one part of Kelly's response (6) and attempts to draw her out to explain, or perhaps justify, what she means.

8. Kelly    Because giving them food handouts doesn't really help them.

Kelly is still being evasive. She begins with a concrete, specific example of help – '. . . giving them food . . .' but then finishes her answer with a non-specific, vague, abstraction – '. . . doesn't really help them.'

9. Teacher    In what way doesn't it really help them?

The teacher again refuses to be put off by the pupil's evasion and reticence. The teacher asks for clarification on the vague part of Kelly's previous response (8).

10. Kelly    Because it doesn't . . . not always.

Kelly persists in being evasive. She repeats the vague part of her answer (8) but qualifies it so that she is no longer making a general claim – 'food handouts never help' to a more qualified claim – 'food handouts don't always help'.

11. Teacher    Can you give an example of when giving poor people food doesn't really help?

The teacher again is not deflected and does not accept Kelly's qualified answer as the best she has to offer. The teacher attempts to remove the vagueness created by the use of abstract statements by asking Kelly for an example.

12. Kelly    If you give them food it just means they are not hungry for a while. A day or two later they will be hungry again and so it doesn't do them any good.

This is a breakthrough response. The persistence of the teacher has paid off. Kelly's thinking is no longer hidden behind unclear abstractions. Kelly provides an example of why she is cautious of the value of aid agencies if their work just results in temporary relief only for the problem to return a short time later.

13. Teacher    How many people agree with what Kelly has said? Giving food to poor people often doesn't help as a day or two later they will be hungry again?

This teacher avoids the temptation to intervene in the discussion and use Kelly's response (12) as an opportunity to tell the class that agencies like Christian Aid do much more than give out emergency relief; they also undertake long-term work to try and solve the underlying causes of poverty. Such interventions are nearly always resented by pupils as they feel 'put down' having been corrected in public. This only makes it more likely that they will be evasive or unwilling to engage in future class discussions.

Instead the teacher tries to involve the rest of the class by asking them about their response to Kelly's comments.

14. Teacher   So do you think Christian Aid is wrong to give food to poor people because a day or two later they will only be hungry again?

The teacher continues to try and engage more pupils in the discussion by asking the class if Kelly's criticism of aid agencies like Christian Aid means that their work is wrong. The teacher avoids didactically telling the pupils that Christian Aid does a lot more than merely defer pain with temporary relief. Instead through questioning the teacher has high expectations that members of the class will themselves make this point during the discussion.

15. Darren   No, you should give poor people food but you need to do more.

Darren spontaneously joins the discussion. His answer suggests that giving out food may be the best that can be done in an emergency but he also suggests that there is also more that needs to be undertaken.

However, Darren doesn't commit himself by saying what this 'more' might be.

16. Teacher   What more do you think should be done to help the very poor?

The teacher again shows higher expectations of pupils than they may at first be willing to demonstrate.

The teacher probes Darren to explain what 'more' things he has in mind which would help the very poor.

17. Darren   You should help poor people to grow their own food, or help them find a job and then they don't have to depend on handouts.

Darren responds by showing a much fuller appreciation of how an aid agency may be effective. It didn't require a didactic intervention by the teacher after all.

Darren and probably quite a few of the other pupils have a sense that aid agencies are vulnerable to moral criticisms if they fail to develop economic self-sufficiency but instead encourage a culture of dependency.

## Pupil generated questions

The questions asked in RE classrooms should not just come from teachers. Pupils should be encouraged to raise their own questions. Indeed one of the characteristics of very able pupils is that they ask pertinent, tricky, probing and original questions. For example:

- If there is only one God why are there so many religions?

- Do animals have souls?

- How do we know Jesus was a real person?

- If God created everything why did he create the AIDS virus?

- Why are many religious people terrorists?

- Why are Catholic priests not allowed to marry?

- If God wants us to believe in him why doesn't he just show himself?

- Do good people who don't believe in God get to go to heaven?

- Before God made the universe what did God do?

- How can Adam and Eve be true if we evolved from apes?

To encourage pupils to ask questions, a space in the classroom can be dedicated as the place where pupils may write good questions which occur to them. The space may be permanently equipped with paper and a pencil on a string. If a good question about faith or belief comes to mind rather than just keeping it to themselves or forgetting about it, pupils are encouraged to write it down and pin it up for public airing in the space provided. The space can be given a novelty element as in the form of a question tree. Pupils pin leaves on which they write their questions onto the tree. Regularly these questions are reviewed and discussed during RE lessons.

## What if . . . ? questions

Good questions in RE stimulate pupils so that they are interested enough to want to answer them. Questions which most attract pupils have about them a freshness or an unusual, quirky edge. Good questions cause pupils to feel enlivened, they spark the mind and so may power thoughts and ideas to take off in new or in unusual directions. Often pupils are asked questions using familiar stems like 'How do . . . ?' or 'What are . . . ?', for example:

- How do Buddhists meditate?

- What are the Sikh Five Ks?

RE questions can be pepped up by using a 'What if . . . ?' stem, for example:

- What if a Buddhist wasn't allowed to meditate?

- What if all Sikhs were forbidden to wear the Five Ks?

- What if all RE in schools was abolished?

- What if they had found Jesus' dead body in the tomb?

- What if an angel appeared to you while you are alone in the middle of the night?

- What if the Qur'an said Muslims had to worship God once a week and not five times a day?

- What if euthanasia was available on demand for everybody over the age of eighty years?

- What if all children with a religious faith went to their own faith school?

'What if . . . ?' questions particularly appeal to very able pupils as they enable them to exercise their imagination and to direct their minds along original and creative lines.

## What would be missed . . . ? questions

Another way to give an interesting twist to questions is to use the stem, 'What would be missed?' This is particularly true of 'Why?' questions. 'Why' questions in RE, although very important, often mystify young people and responses are frequently disappointing. Phrasing such questions using the stem, 'What would be missed?' often enables pupils to see the issue in a new light and come up with a much more productive response.

To illustrate this point imagine asking a 12-year-old, 'Why do you play football?' The young player might struggle to make a coherent response. Playing football seems like such a self-evidently enjoyable thing to do that to ask 'Why?' is likely to leave our young player uncertain as to how to respond. 'Because I like it!' surely should be a good enough answer.

However, if the question was, 'What would you miss if you didn't play football?' the question becomes a good deal less puzzling. Our imaginary 12-year-old might talk about the thrill of winning, or about the comradeship of being part of a team, or about the health benefits of running about, or the sense of satisfaction gained when one does well at something which is difficult like crossing a ball from the wing, going round a player with a body swerve, or making a tackle.

Similarly 'What would be missed . . . ?' questions in RE often enable pupils to make a more interesting response. Consider the following examples:

- What would be missed if a Muslim never went on hajj?

- What would be missed if a Christian never prayed?

- What would be missed if Jewish people didn't have a written Holy Scripture?

- What would be missed if Hindus had no images of the deity?

- What would be missed if a Christian couldn't receive Holy Communion?

- What would be missed if funerals or ceremonies did not take place when a person died?

- What would be missed if Jesus had never been born?

# Alternatives to writing – formal debate

Formal debate is comparatively underused in the RE classroom. However, as a strategy for developing thinking and reasoning skills in RE, and as a valuable alternative to writing, debating has a great deal to offer. The basic format of an RE debate is identical to any other debate. A debate consists of two teams. One team proposes a motion and the other team opposes the motion. The size of a team may vary but often there are four pupils in each team, making a total of eight pupils. Although these eight pupils have an important role, it is essential to ensure that all the other members of the class, as much as possible, are also engaged in the debate. They should not have the impression that they just sit around as an attentive audience and have a vote at the end.

Two speakers in each team are given enough time to make a developed, persuasive case. Normally three to four minutes is sufficient. The two other speakers in each team are given enough time to present counter-assignments, or make supplementary arguments. Usually these speakers are allowed a maximum of one minute. The timing of these contributions are strictly controlled. No one is allowed to go over time and indulge themselves in long-winded speeches.

Once the eight main speakers have presented their case the motion is thrown open for the whole class to debate. Contributions from the floor of the house should be expected. They should not be treated as a cursory possibility which may or may not happen. Teachers do have to be patient and endure what might seem like an embarrassing silence while the first pupil plucks up the courage to speak. However, patience nearly always pays off. Eventually, someone will speak and usually others will then follow.

An RE debate clearly must have a motion which has something to do with religion, but the other distinctive characteristic of an RE debate is that there is a real attempt to reduce as much as possible the adversarial nature of debate.

## Motions for an RE debate

A good debating topic in RE shouldn't be tame or flat. To generate interest a good debating topic usually has a spiky, contentious edge. A recent event in the news can also form the basis of a motion which has a contemporary relevance and an added frisson.

Possible motions for an RE debate might include:

### This house believes . . .

- the Boxing Day tsunami shows us that the compassionate God of the Bible and the Qur'an does not exist.
- authors of books and plays have a right to be offensive about religion.
- the Muslim countries are right to forbid beauty queen contests.
- religious objections to birth control in developing countries are a harmful intrusion.

- teaching children to believe in hell is a form of child abuse.
- religion has brought humankind more peace than war.
- cloning human cells for research purposes is a dangerous example of humans 'playing God'.
- religion should be banned from all state-funded schools in Britain.
- it is Islamic regimes, not the West, that have largely oppressed Muslims.
- the evidence for the resurrection of Jesus is substantial and convincing.

## Non-adversarial debate

There is a great deal more educational value if participants understand an RE debate to be essentially non-adversarial and non-competitive. Although students will propose and counter arguments, the central principle of an RE debate is to throw light on a subject through public debate. It is not about scoring points off the opposition by sophistry, heightened passion or a show of clever repartee. An RE debate should be based on prepared arguments. Students should have had an opportunity to research the evidence and consider their arguments to support their case. Although being inventive and adapting an argument does come into it, an RE debate is not primarily a demonstration of 'thinking on your feet' or putting up a convincing case at a moment's notice.

The main principles governing an RE debate are:

- mutual respect
- good humour
- informed knowledge and information
- consistency and clarity of thought.

Students should ensure that they avoid:

- merely mocking the opposition
- using distorted or unfounded information
- using emotional or violent language
- being offensive, personal or patronising.

The debate will usually be concluded with a vote so that students may vote for the motion, or against it, or may choose to abstain. However, all the students involved should understand that the vote is about the motion being debated. It is not about voting for the team that appears to have put on the best debating performance. No team should feel that they 'lost the debate' or that in any sense they have been knocked out of a competition.

## Local authority RE debate

Some local authorities, for example Dudley MBC, encourage religious debate by making available the local council debating chambers. Such a venue provides an added gravitas and a sense of occasion to the event. A local authority organised debate may well pit one school's debating team against a team from another school. Even if this is the arrangement the emphasis must still be on intelligent and thoughtful contributions and not on deploying dubious rhetorical devices in the belief that debating is about putting on a clever show.

## Changes in the field of study

It may already be obvious that none of the suggested motions for RE debates relate to topics which have characterised much of RE for the past thirty years. Topics such as worship, leaders of religions, religious festivals, holy books, places of pilgrimage and initiation ceremonies have for almost three decades often been a major feature of RE schemes of work. The emphasis has tended to be on what might be described as the phenomena of religion.

By aiming in lessons to explore what these obvious manifestations of religion mean and in what sense they have meaning or relevance for us today, it is possible to create challenging RE which makes substantial demands upon the very able child. As Lat Blaylock, the editor of *RE Today*, has put it, the idea is to 'use the ultimate or fundamental questions that lie below the surface of religious practice to open the ways in which pupils learn from religion'. In other words the aim is not that young people learn lots of facts about, say, funeral rites but to use the phenomenon of funeral rites as a springboard to consider 'issues of purpose in life'.

Although this approach to RE is undoubtedly challenging and rewarding, one of the questions asked of RE in recent years is: if an important part of the intention is to direct the minds of young people towards 'ultimate or fundamental questions' why take such a circuitous route? Why draw young people's attention to the phenomenon of religion? Instead why not challenge students with the significant 'big questions' more directly? Increasingly many teachers of RE in Key Stage 4, but also in Key Stage 3, are devoting less time to the phenomena of religion approach. Instead it is possible to see a change in the field of study towards an RE which is more about issues and ideas. The phenomena of religion approach has not disappeared but more time is being given to contemporary issues, moral dilemmas and what might be called philosophy of religion.

This shift of emphasis in RE is reflected in *The Non-Statutory National Framework for Religious Education* (DFES/QCA 2004). In the Breadth of Study section for Key Stage 3 (p. 29), there are eight themes:

- beliefs and concepts: the key ideas and questions of meaning in religions and beliefs, including issues related to God, truth, the world, human life, and life after death
- authority: different sources of authority and how they inform believers' lives

- religion and science: issues of truth, explanation, meaning and purpose

- expressions of spirituality: how and why human self-understanding and experiences are expressed in a variety of forms

- ethics and relationships: questions and influences that inform ethical and moral choices, including forgiveness and issues of good and evil

- rights and responsibilities: what religions and beliefs say about human rights and responsibilities, social justice and citizenship

- global issues: what religions and beliefs say about health, wealth, war, animal rights and the environment

- interfaith dialogue: a study of relationships, conflicts and collaboration within and between religion and beliefs.

## 'Issues and ideas' programme

All of these themes suggest a move away from a 'phenomena of religion' scheme of work. Themes like worship, pilgrimage, sacred places and symbols still feature in Key Stage 2. However in Key Stage 3 the themes are much more overtly focused on what is sometimes called an 'issues and ideas' programme. This is partly to ensure that pupils in Key Stage 3 do not merely repeat tasks which they were capable of undertaking, and indeed in some cases did undertake in Key Stage 2. It is also an attempt to drive up the level of challenge for all students in Key Stage 3, including a higher level of challenge for very able pupils.

In order to ensure that a higher level of challenge is introduced into Key Stage 3 RE it is vital that an 'issues and ideas' programme is not treated as simply an alternative body of knowledge which is to be transmitted to young people. For example, imagine that as part of a 'global issues' theme young people are taught what Buddhists, Muslims and Christians have said about animal rights. Pupils might listen to the teacher's account, or read about it in a book or on various internet sites, following which pupils are asked, 'What might a Buddhist say about whether animals have rights?' or 'Compare what Muslims and Christians say about whether animals have rights'. Such an activity essentially engages the pupils in a non-demanding recall assignment. The fact that they are recalling the 'issues and ideas' of others doesn't significantly raise the level of challenge compared with recalling what Christians might do during a Confirmation service or what Muslims might do during the fast of Ramadan. Replacing a 'phenomena of religion' programme with a more 'issues and ideas' programme does not guarantee a higher level of challenge in the classroom if the teaching strategy remains largely didactic.

An 'issues and ideas' RE programme only raises the level of challenge if pupils are given tasks which require them to think and make judgements. For example, pupils may be asked to:

- analyse and explain the structure of an argument

- explain the strengths or weaknesses of a set of ideas

- evaluate the evidence for a belief

- originate, clarify or strengthen an argument.

RE of this form is much more evident in departments which have shifted towards a philosophy of religion programme.

## Philosophy of religion

Philosophy of religion, certainly in the West, has mainly been concerned with questions like:

- Does God exist?

- If there is a God why is there evil in the world?

- Is there a life after death?

- Do we have souls?

- Do miracles really happen?

If we take into account the close relationship between ethical theory and religious faith, other questions may also be addressed in a philosophy of religion programme, for example:

- Is what is good independent of God?

- Is what is good whatever God says is good?

- Does the Golden Rule answer all moral problems?

- Is it necessary to believe in God to be good?

- If there is no God is our sense of right or wrong just based on our personal feelings?

All of these questions could form the basis of a number of very stimulating and challenging RE topics. Helping young people to become aware of philosophical ideas features strongly in *The Non-Statutory National Framework for Religious Education*. The framework makes it clear that philosophy has a very important place in Key Stage 3 RE. Philosophy of religion is not so lofty that it is only suitable for older students in Key Stage 4, or post-16. However, in order to get the most out of a philosophy of religion programme, pupils should not simply be engaged in a sort of historical enquiry into what some great thinkers of the past have said. Personalising arguments and providing an historical context is important and can be an aid to learning. However, there is a real difference in a student who can answer the question, 'Who in the thirteenth century wrote a famous cosmological argument for the existence of God?' in contrast to the student who can undertake the task, 'Explain the cosmological argument for the existence of God.' Being able to answer the first question shows a historical knowledge. Being able to undertake the second task demonstrates the much more demanding ability to comprehend philosophical concepts and arguments.

## Teaching formally how to structure an argument

Often, as part of a philosophy of religion programme students are asked to consider a question, for example, 'Must there be a God to explain how the world began?' Or alternatively students may be invited to consider a point of view expressed in the form of a quotation, for example, 'The world must have been made by God.' Students are then asked to respond to the question or quote by being asked, 'What do you think?' or 'Do you agree?' Often, in order to make it clear that a simple 'Yes' or 'No' answer won't do, students are asked to 'Give reasons to support your answer.'

Activities of this sort are based on the belief that asking students, 'What do you think?' or inviting them to 'give reasons' improves their ability to think and provide reasons. This is not a totally unfounded belief. However, often young people are given very little guidance as to what a good 'reason' might look like or very little practical help on how an argument might be structured in order to best reflect their thinking.

For pupils to become really skilled at 'thinking' and 'giving reasons' it is possible and desirable to teach young people more directly what exactly a 'reason' is and how a reasoned argument might be constructed. For example, in order to help young people to improve their ability to construct a persuasive argument, pupils might be shown examples of what a philosophical or ethical argument looks like and to formally study what the writer has done to try and make the argument persuasive.

As an example of this pupils might be asked to look at a simplified version of William Paley's design argument for God.

### William Paley's design argument

> All round us we see in nature a world that has been designed. Look at a simple daisy and you will see petals neatly arranged around a circular bud. Can anyone seriously imagine that such a symmetrical design just happens by accident? The daisy shows the marks of having been designed. Imagine in the middle of nowhere you came across a watch. If you looked at how all the wheels and cogs are connected together you would have to say, 'This is no accident. Somebody has designed this. A watch must have a watchmaker.' The neat pattern of a daisy, the shape of a fish's tail, the intricate parts that make up the human eye; all these things have the marks of design. Design doesn't just happen by accident. Design must have a designer. That designer is God.

Pupils might be asked to study the passage carefully and suggest, 'How has the writer tried to make the argument convincing?' Or, alternatively pupils might be asked to study the text carefully and explain how the writer has:

- made use of analogy to clarify the argument

- avoided only abstract statements by using examples

- made use of a rhetorical question to give the argument 'punch'.

Pupils might study other examples of how an analogy might be used to make an argument more vivid and persuasive. They then might be asked to practise writing an argument of their own making use of analogy to give their argument added life and power.

## Teaching formally how to reason

Alongside the technique of asking pupils to 'give your reasons', helping very able pupils to achieve a deeper grasp of what a 'reason' is and that some reasons may be better than others may be achieved by a similar more formal and direct way. The relative merits of different reasons, or perhaps even a hierarchy of reasons, can be usefully explained to young people. Particularly in the area of ethical discussion reasons can be helpfully categorised into three main groups: lower order reasons which are least effective; middle order reasons; and the most effective category of reasons, higher order reasons.

The following table illustrates this idea of a hierarchy of reasons using the moral question, 'Is stealing wrong?' as an example.

| 'Stealing is wrong because . . .' | |
| --- | --- |
| *Higher order reasons which have a broader appeal* | |
| principles or rights | '. . . you should respect other people's right to have things if you want other people to respect your right to have things.' |
| social consequences | '. . . everything could get out of hand and people would just be stealing from each other all the time.' |
| *Middle order reasons* | |
| secular authority | '. . . it is against the law.' |
| religious authority | '. . . it says so in the Bible.' |
| limited authority | '. . . my Mum says it's wrong.' |
| *Lower order reasons, least persuasive* | |
| personal consequence | '. . . people might not like you.' |
| expediency | '. . . you might get found out.' |
| circular | '. . . you shouldn't do it.' |

By being made familiar directly with higher order reasons pupils are more likely to understand what a 'good reason' is like and so are more likely to be able to recognise and make use of good reasons when writing or discussing.

The careful analysis of arguments, noting their strengths and weaknesses, can also enable young people to become more aware of errors in their own thinking and more sensitive to flaws in the arguments presented by others. For example:

| | |
|---|---|
| hidden assumptions | As the world has been designed it follows that it was designed by one God. |
| generalising from particular | Some members of the Church object to female priests hence the Church is sexist. |
| anecdotal claims | My sister's teenage marriage worked so teenage marriage does work. |
| recognising contradictions | I believe in immortality but there is no life after death. |
| ambiguous language | Darwin's theory of evolution is just a theory. |
| emotive language | Day in day out, people are mopping up the blood of innocent creatures that are the victims of sick animal abusers. |
| false premise | For everything there is an opposite. So it follows, if God rewards some people, He must also punish others. |

In summary then, the challenging RE classroom in which all pupils, including the very able pupil, can flourish may well be one in which the field of study has taken a significant shift. Particularly from Key Stage 3 onwards the emphasis is not so much on the observable phenomena of religion. Instead, the move is towards confronting in the classroom some of the fundamental questions which life and religion pose and which have traditionally been asked by philosophy of religion.

Pupils gain from this study not simply knowledge of what the 'greats' have said in the past but an insight into how an argument may be legitimately constructed, how an argument may be flawed, how evidence and reasons may be presented and how arguments may be appropriately countered using reason and courtesy. By doing so pupils clarify their own thinking and arrive at a much more reasoned response to religion and belief. They are more aware of the merits but also of the weaknesses in the positions they adopt and are similarly aware of the merits and weaknesses of alternative views.

## Summary

- Plan and ask questions of substance, encourage pupils to generate questions.
- Raise the level of challenge through an 'issues and ideas' programme.
- Teach formally what reasons are and how effective arguments may be structured.

**CHAPTER 6**

# Supporting the work of more able pupils

- Gifted children with special needs
- The school library and external agencies
- Teaching assistants and mentoring

## Gifted children with special needs

The received wisdom is that a child that is very able in RE is highly motivated. The widespread assumption is that very able children are naturally inquisitive, have retentive minds and enjoy learning. The truth is that some very able pupils can have an extraordinary flair for RE but can also have very real learning difficulties. Being gifted in RE but also having to struggle with learning difficulties is not a contradiction. Teachers of RE need to be sensitive to the needs of individual pupils who have particular learning difficulties which may require quite specific tailored support.

Learning difficulties which can impact on the progress of gifted children can take many different forms. The following section discusses just four learning difficulties which classroom teachers are most likely to encounter:

- Asperger syndrome

- dyslexia

- managing disruptive behaviour

- sensory impairment.

## Asperger syndrome

Asperger syndrome is well known as a condition whereby pupils can show an impaired flexibility in thinking and understanding and yet young people with this condition may also possess a very high level of intelligence and show remarkable powers of cognition. The syndrome tends to affect more boys than girls. Usually, it shows itself in three main ways:

- **social interaction** – pupils with Asperger syndrome are sometimes unable to pick up on social cues or learn social norms and this affects their ability to interact socially with others. A pupil may never offer eye contact. They may appear socially cut off and without friends.

- **social communication** – a pupil may tend to talk in a monotone, using little modulation. Their voice may sound flat and without appropriate emotion. They may have a very literal understanding of language. For example, a pupil with Asperger syndrome may be horrified to hear a teacher say, 'Let's pick your brains', the words seemingly conjuring up a frightening intrusion into the pupil's skull.

- **social imagination** – pupils with Asperger syndrome often need to have fixed routines which they know and can anticipate. They are often good at learning facts but have difficulty with abstract concepts.

As a pupil with Asperger syndrome may lack empathy and the ability to appreciate the emotions and feelings of others, children with the syndrome might be expected to show little ability in RE. However, this is not necessarily the case. The way in which the syndrome manifests itself in individuals varies enormously. While some pupils with the syndrome may struggle to achieve a grasp of the subject beyond mere factual recall, other pupils, even though their emotional response to others is very limited, may have a very strong intellectual grasp of aspects of the subject. Particularly when the subject matter is focused on ideas rather than emotions, as for example may be true in philosophy of religion, pupils with the syndrome can excel.

A pupil with Asperger syndrome, for example, may show a meticulous attention to detail when looking at different theodicies associated with the problem of evil. The ability to be emotionally disengaged while working with ideas may in fact be an advantage enabling the pupil to recognise false premises, hidden assumptions or flawed reasoning. Some pupils with the syndrome are not only able to apply a scalpel-like mind to weaknesses in the arguments of others, they are able, more positively, to be creative and original thinkers. Given the opportunity some pupils with Asperger syndrome are able to construct a detailed and rigorously consistent line of logical deduction. Some are able to overcome their reservations about unfamiliar settings or engaging with others and become formidable members of a debating team or lead members of a discussion group.

## Dyslexia

There is no one definition of dyslexia or one identified cause. The term is used to describe pupils who have difficulty with words. That may involve a very specific difficulty with reading, writing or spelling, or a general difficulty with all of these skills. A young person may be highly gifted in RE but their ability is only evident when they speak, for example, when responding to or raising questions, or in classroom discussions or debates.

However, if an RE classroom is dominated by the teacher's discourse and challenging assignments are invariably written assignments it is possible that the ability of a very able, but dyslexic, child may remain undetected. The child will always find themselves being asked to work in a medium which causes them difficulty. For example, their written work may be messy, littered with crossing outs, and filled with confused or unintelligible spelling. Indeed, their written work may be so incomprehensible that a busy teacher of RE simply does not have the time to decipher the work. Any depth of understanding or quality of thinking is simply not noticed. Instead the work may be returned to the pupil with a plea rather than helpful guidance or diagnosis, e.g. 'Try to keep your work neater'. Such a comment reflects the problem the teacher is experiencing but doesn't address the difficulties the child is having.

### RE and writing

Whether or not a child has evident difficulty with writing, the writing of all young people in RE lessons can be improved if pupils are encouraged to draft and redraft their work. Some people do have the ability to put down on paper their thoughts and ideas in a flawless first draft. However, for most of us writing is a process, often a painful one, involving false starts, major blunders and many changes of mind. Expecting young people to be able to undertake a complicated writing assignment which shows psychological, moral, social or theological insight into an aspect of religion and to achieve a perfect product in a single draft while sitting in a classroom is extravagantly optimistic.

### The loose-leaf folder

Alternatively, young people should be encouraged to think of writing activities as work which can be edited and revised several times. Some teachers of RE have abandoned the exercise book in favour of a loose-leaf folder. This enables pupils to store final drafts which can be a source of pride, instead of having to turn through pages of an exercise book only to be reminded of past failures.

### Word processing

Pupils should also be encouraged to word process their writing. This not only enables young people to create a high quality final product, it is of immense help as work passes through its various stages of editing, erasing and refining.

### Context and purpose

Pupils also find it easier if a writing activity is set into a context so that pupils have a sense of the purpose of the writing and also a sense of who the audience might be. Asking pupils to 'Explain what the Five Ks symbolise' is a somewhat predictable and flat assignment. It also has the whiff of being a mere academic exercise which has no relevance in the real world. Alternatively, the assignment may be presented in the following way.

The following letter appeared in 'The Letters' page of a local newspaper.

## Bit of banter?

The fuss made by the Sikh gentleman who complained that people at work were making 'jokey' comments about him wearing the turban and other things connected to his religion was ridiculous. A bit of banter at work should just be laughed off. Is the world now so politically correct that we can't be a bit cheeky about what is on somebody's head?

As for wearing a knife, that's just wrong. Don't try and pretend to me it's not a knife, by calling it a kirpan and claiming it's just a symbol. The fact is, it's a dangerous weapon and nobody should be carrying a weapon.

Surely it's time Sikhs questioned whether they really need to wear things like the comb and the steel wristband which they have. Why try to stand out and go out of your way to look different? Isn't it time for people to make more of an effort to fit in?

M. Y. Pinooni

- Write a letter of your own to the newspaper putting the case against M. Y. Pinooni.
- Your letter should be about 150–220 words.
- Use respectful language.
- Research the Sikh Five Ks, particularly why Sikhs wear the Five Ks, so that your information is accurate.

By presenting the activity in this way, it no longer resembles an academic exercise. The activity now has a degree of reality and purpose about it so that the value to pupils of developing their writing skills becomes more evident. The activity also suggests the sort of audience and hence the style the pupils might adopt. For example, a letter to a newspaper's readers' letter page needs to be brief and 'to the point' and yet accurate and persuasive. Also, by making available the realistic but fictitious opinion of M. Y. Pinooni, pupils' thinking may be stimulated. It provides pupils with some ideas on which they can hang their own comments and so begins to offer the pupils a structure around which they can build their response, without the rather deadening effect of a formal writing frame.

### Diagnostic analysis

However, for some gifted children with writing difficulties in order for them to make effective progress a proper diagnostic analysis may have to be made. In many cases the problem is unlikely to be simply a problem with writing in RE but writing generally. To deal with the issue effectively a diagnostic analysis would normally mean that the school, not simply the RE department, needs to find out what an individual child does when they are asked to write. For example:

- How does the child plan their work?

- How does the child set about composition?

- What sort of errors does the child make when writing?

- Does the child write in short and repetitious sentences?

- Does the child write in long clumsy sentences using too many conjunctions?

- Does the child read back their work in order to correct it?

- Is the main problem to do with the quality of handwriting and not composition?

- Does the child show skills when undertaking descriptive writing but weaknesses when attempting persuasive or discursive writing?

When the problem has been properly diagnosed the teacher can then focus attention on what the child is doing wrong. For example, if a very able child has real difficulties with putting their own views down on paper in a persuasive form, the teacher may help the child by modelling how an effective piece of persuasive writing can be created. This may involve helping the child to think about and practise:

- identifying a persuasive reason

- how a line of argument might be developed and reinforced

- using rhetorical questions to give punch to an argument

- using analogy to bring an argument alive and give it clarity

- how arguments to the contrary can be introduced

- how emotive or disrespectful language may mar an argument.

## Spelling

Having real difficulty with spelling is often seen as a main characteristic of dyslexia. Poor spelling may be due to a pupil persistently confusing similarly shaped letters, for example, m/w, p/q, b/d, n/u. However, this is not the only way in which a pupil may struggle with spelling. A pupil may have outstanding ability in RE, they may love words, they may have a huge vocabulary of religious terms, and yet they seem blind to the errors they make when they attempt to spell. Such a problem can often result in pupils becoming reluctant writers. Even though their writing may be excellent, in order to avoid the embarrassment of revealing their difficulty with spelling, very able pupils may:

- avoid writing

- write only the minimum

- disguise their poor spelling with unintelligible handwriting

- avoid using more expressive or specialist words which they suspect they will spell incorrectly

- adopt a limited vocabulary restricting themselves to words which they are confident they can spell correctly.

The assumption is often made that very able children, particularly if they read a lot, or if they see words which they spell incorrectly frequently enough, eventually will crack the problem and get the hang of it. This is not always true. Some pupils have such a weak visual memory for words that the problems they experience with spelling simply do not go away. The problem can persist into adult life with individuals failing to confront the difficulty they have with spelling. Rather than admit and attempt to tackle the problem, many people find more sophisticated ways of trying to cover it up and pretend it is not an issue.

### Specialist vocabulary in RE

It is also true that in RE young people will encounter many specialist words which are often transliterations from Arabic, Greek, Hebrew, Sanskrit, Punjabi and other languages. The preferred way in which some of these words should be transliterated into English may result in unusual letter combinations which do not obey many of the rules which good spellers often make use of. For example, there is no 'u' following the use of the letter 'q' in the word which refers to the direction of prayer used by Muslims – *qibla*. The words *Panj kakke* which denotes the Five Ks in Sikhism contains the unusual letter combinations 'nj' and 'kk'.

Use is also made of the apostrophe not to indicate, as might be expected, possession or a dropped letter. Instead the apostrophe may appear in the middle of a word as it may represent a sound which has no equivalence in English or it may represent no sound at all in the form of a glottal stop, for example Qur'an and Rak'ah. Good spellers that have a strong visual memory for words can quickly learn these words after being acquainted with them on only one or two occasions. However, poor spellers may see these words hundreds of times. They may have no problem reading them or using them in classroom discussions. Yet, when they attempt to spell them the combination of letters evades them and they are left frustrated.

### Strategies to help improve spelling

Trying to help such pupils improve their spelling by advising them to 'check your spelling' or highlighting their error by writing 'sp' in the margin, or making them do spelling corrections by copying the word many times, will make no difference. Indeed it may simply add to their frustration. Instead the problem has to be tackled seriously and systematically:

- Help the pupil to confront the problem by drawing up together a list of words the pupil frequently misspells.

- Systematically target a word. Encourage the pupil to make an active effort to remember every detail of the targeted word. Study how the word should be spelt but also encourage the student to study how they tend to misspell the word. Explain to the pupils that they should not rely on simply looking at a targeted word for it to become embedded in their memory. Pupils with spelling difficulties will usually need to do more than just persistently look at a word. Often they will need to learn the words by eye, ear and hand. This means they will need to see the word, say the word and feel the word as they actually write it. This will usually take the form of a 'look, say, cover and write' strategy.

- Give the pupils a sense of achievement by making use of a progress chart on which they can record the number of new words learnt each week.

- Avoid frustration when writing: encourage pupils to make use of electronic spellcheckers.

## Managing disruptive behaviour

### Behavioural, emotional and social difficulties (BESD)

Although often associated with pupils with less ability, young people with behavioural, emotional and social difficulties (BESD) can be seen across the whole ability range including the very able. A young person may be easily angered, physically and verbally aggressive, restless and inattentive and yet may be highly intelligent and be extraordinarily gifted, or have the potential to be extraordinarily gifted in RE. Being gifted also does not exclude pupils that have attention deficit hyperactivity disorder (ADHD) and pupils that have attention deficit disorder without hyperactivity (ADD).

A young person of high ability is not immune to the possibility that their life outside school may be highly fractured. Pupils may bring into the classroom frustrations and anxieties generated by events experienced outside the school environment. Regretfully, young people may find themselves knowing in their personal lives all too closely hurt, anger and disappointment. It is little wonder then that for some children when they walk into any classroom, whatever the subject, the expectation that they should be alert, attentive and engaged is one which they may miserably fail to achieve. Being aware of a child's personal circumstances can throw a bright light on a child's behaviour and can be a major factor in helping a teacher decide how a child might best be supported.

### Attention deficit and hyperactivity disorder (ADHD)

As well as the difficulties some young people have to cope with arising from their home environment, there is increasing evidence which suggests that the impulsive behaviour of some young people diagnosed with ADHD has nothing to do with troubled homes. Based on evidence derived from PET and MRI brain scanning, young people with ADHD are widely thought by many specialists in the field to have an imbalance in their brain's neurotransmitter chemicals. This imbalance in the brain's chemistry means that the brain has difficulty transmitting the signals which prevent unwise behaviour.

This feature of the brain's functioning affects the individual's ability to regulate their own behaviour. It does not directly affect an individual's cognitive skills, although, of course, indirectly it can have a huge effect on a child's ability to sit still and be cooperative which can be so important in a learning environment. In other words, a child with ADHD may present to the world an inattentive and overactive temperament, which is difficult to teach, but behind the frustrating behaviour there may be a very able child.

### Treating ADHD

ADHD is a long-term condition which mostly affects boys. However, girls are not immune to the condition. The treatment of young people with ADHD partly involves giving advice on understanding their condition, behavioural advice but also increasing use is being made of stimulant medication.

Stimulant medication, for example, prescribing ritalin or dexamphetamine, enables a child to exercise more effective control of their own behaviour. Medical treatment using stimulants does not dope children to subdue behaviour adults don't like. Its purpose is to help the brain's poorly functioning chemical transmitters do their normal job more effectively, which is to put the brakes on impulsive behaviour.

### A 'behaviour profile'

In order to make effective progress with a pupil who has emotional and behaviour difficulties it often helps to first undertake a proper analysis of their behaviour. For a child that has ADHD and has been diagnosed as being in need of stimulant medication high priority must be given to ensuring medication is available. However, analysing the circumstances in which impulsive or aggressive behaviour may arise can be of help. Such an analysis is called a 'behaviour profile'. The purpose of such an analysis is to see if there is any pattern to a child's behaviour. For example, is a child having difficulty controlling their behaviour generally throughout the school or is it only an issue which arises during RE lessons? Is there a pattern of misbehaviour associated with certain other pupils or does it coincide with lessons following time spent mingling with other pupils in the playground?

If such a pattern can be detected, is there a school behaviour policy in place which can tackle the problem and help the child to improve their behaviour? If a child's disruptive behaviour is mainly limited to the RE classroom a number of reasons for this might have to be considered.

### Poor experience of the subject

The pupil may have had a poor experience of the subject. Perhaps their previous teacher of RE suffered long-term illness and they had unsatisfactory supply and cover staff. Or maybe their previous teacher of RE was overbearing and used the subject as an opportunity to air only their own beliefs. Because of this the child has developed a low opinion of the subject and now fails to treat it seriously.

### Poor teaching strategies

The child may find the teaching strategies too predictable and lacking in challenge. Some very able children are simply bored by lessons and mentally abscond by daydreaming. Some choose to spice up dull lessons by baiting the teacher. Often this takes the form of low level disruption, for example, persistent verbal asides or 'jokey' questions not relevant to the topic being discussed. For example, in the middle of a lesson about enlightenment in Buddhism a pupil asks, 'Please, Miss, how do we know Mary was a virgin?'

### Irrelevant scheme of work

Even though the teaching strategies may be well designed the scheme of work, from the point of view of an able child, may lack any relevance or purpose. For example, a series of lessons on the Old Testament patriarchs might be of great interest to the teacher or even to some pupils, but a child that is very able might be completely switched off and feel 'what's the point?'

### Poor teacher/pupil relationship

Very able children are not necessarily angels. An able child may sense a teacher's insecurity or may take advantage by mocking a teacher's mannerisms or habits of speech. The child may not have a problem with RE but they may take a dislike to, or develop a poor relationship with, an individual teacher of RE.

### Classroom management

There are no unique rules which apply to a teacher of RE about how to manage a gifted child that has ADHD or some other form of emotional and behavioural problem. The points listed below could equally apply to a teacher of English, history, or indeed a teacher of any subject.

## Points on classroom management

### Avoid using reactive power

If a child suddenly becomes aggressive, perhaps arising from an incident involving another pupil, avoid simply shouting at the child and telling them to behave. Shouting at a child may seem like the quickest and easiest method to hand. Many teachers believe that by aggressively raising the voice the teacher regains their authority and shows that they are 'in charge'. However, shouting at children usually only results in more tension and hostility in the classroom. It sours the relationship needed in the classroom to ensure effective learning.

### Remain calm

If a child is disruptive, perhaps by using verbal interruptions or by becoming aggressive, remain calm and talk calmly. Speak clearly but not loudly. Avoid being sarcastic, rude or patronising, e.g. 'Have you quite finished behaving like a baby? Are you going to listen now? That would make a nice change.' Be assertive but not aggressive.

### Focus on primary behaviour

When challenged about their behaviour, for example, for being inattentive or off task, a child may become resentful and register their irritation by subsequent but secondary forms of challenging behaviour, for example, answering back. The teacher should stay focused on the primary behaviour and not become sidetracked by the secondary behaviour.

### Rule reinforcement

Avoid entering into discussions about what is, or what is not, acceptable behaviour, or discussions about why a child needs to modify their behaviour. Publicly nagging a pupil about their behaviour detracts from the main aim of the lesson, which is about learning. Make your point about behaviour by reference to a rule. Rule reinforcement should be a short and clear statement, for example, 'Remember the rule, Carol – do not interrupt when someone else is speaking, thank you'. Make it clear that compliance with the rule is a requirement not a request.

### Tactical withdrawal

Having spoken to a child about their behaviour tactically withdraw to avoid confrontation. Poor behaviour is often attention seeking. Avoid rewarding poor behaviour or increasing the chances of additional confrontation by physically moving away and giving your attention to something else.

### Catch pupils being good

Attempt to be positive and not just negative in the classroom by always seeming to be nagging pupils or ticking them off. Send out a clear signal that pupils will not only get your attention if they misbehave. Be alert to things which pupils do which are positive and let them know that you approve. For example, 'That's an excellent point, Raymond. Thanks for putting your hand up.' 'This group is doing well. One person is taking notes and everybody is contributing.' Verbal encouragement is often sufficient but avoid sounding gushy or insincere. Be particularly alert to the child that has difficulty behaving and give them verbal rewards if they show only slight signs of improving: 'Lee has got his biro out and has made a start. Good job, Lee.'

### Encourage learning not just improve behaviour

If a child is very able but has emotional or behavioural problems give them opportunities to cool off. Follow up afterwards giving the child encouragement and ideas to stimulate their learning and not just improve their behaviour. For example, make a point of finding them outside the classroom. Hand them a printout from a website or lend them a book saying, 'I saw this the other day, Jade, and thought of you.'

### Get to know the whole child

Show children that you are human and that you are interested in them as individual people not just as RE learning machines. Take an interest in what football team they support, music they play, TV programmes they watch and let them know you remember and care about their lives outside school. For example, as you meet or pass young people in the corridor or around the school make a point of acknowledging them saying things like 'Good morning, Geoff, the Harriers did well again on Saturday.' 'Hi, Lucy, how's your arm? Are you on the mend?'

## Sensory impairment

Teaching very able children that have some form of sensory impairment is not at all uncommon. Teachers are fairly likely to encounter very able young people that have a hearing, a visual or perhaps a mobility impairment.

### *Hearing impairment*

It is very easy for a young person with a hearing impairment to feel that they are missing out and are not fully involved in lessons, particularly if a great deal of the really challenging work in an RE classroom arises in the form of class discussion and debate. Teachers should attempt to help very able young people with a hearing impairment by:

- ensuring that the child is in the best seating position to be able to hear all that is going on

- make use of any specialist personal radio-mike system

- switch off any apparatus which gives rise to unnecessary extraneous sound, e.g. the hum of an inkjet printer or an OHP

- ensure that the child can see the teacher's face so that they can pick up facial expressions or perhaps lip read

- during discussions insist that only one pupil speaks at a time and indicate the speaker

- provide a written copy of key questions, assignments or a list of significant words which are being introduced in the course of the lesson

- consider making use of a learning partner to provide additional support

- consider arranging regular meetings with a very able child as a mentor to discuss their progress in RE and whether their learning experience can be improved.

### *Visual impairment*

When teaching a very able child that has a visual impairment the following ideas should be considered:

- provide an enlarged print copy of written text

- make use of any specialist equipment, e.g. enlarged print dictionaries, screen reader software, interactive whiteboard, magnification lens

- inform the pupil if the layout of the room has been changed and ensure the walk area is not obstructed

- ensure that the pupil is in the optimum position to see what is taking place in a lesson

- avoid vague directional statements like 'this', 'here' or 'over there'

- discuss with the child whether they wish to have a sighted partner to work with on a fairly regular basis.

## Physical disability

When teaching very able pupils that have a physical disability, in addition to some of points already made such as ensuring that there are no obstructions in movement areas, the following additional suggestions should also be borne in mind:

- allow the pupil to leave the lesson early to avoid busy corridors

- sit beside a wheelchair user so that your eyes are at a similar level

- don't assume that a wheelchair user, or a person with a physical disability, must need help to access resources or equipment; having a sense of independence is often important

- however, be alert in case the pupil does need assistance

- give consideration to how the pupil can fully participate in learning activities like role-play, group work, drama and out-of-school visits

- find out what special arrangements examination boards allow for pupils with sensory or physical impairment, e.g. additional time, rest breaks

- establish a procedure by which a pupil can catch up if they miss a lesson, or a number of lessons, due to medical or physiotherapy appointments

- be sensitive to a pupil if they are experiencing fatigue.

## High expectations

Above all it is important to maintain high expectations. Encourage pupils to strive to do their best and avoid any suggestion that they are doing okay given their impairment. Be imaginative and flexible when setting tasks and assignments. For example, an assignment for a child with a mobility impairment may be modified so that it does not involve physically visiting a local place of worship. Instead the child may wish to study how a place of worship is using its website to preach its message and support members of the community.

However, avoid making assumptions. Discuss and listen to what a child has to say. For example, encouraging a very able child with a visual impairment to undertake a study of how contemporary people with faith have responded to their loss of sight might be of immense interest and a fascinating opportunity for the child. However, another equally able child also with a visual impairment might be completely uninterested by such an assignment regarding it as well intentioned but the product of rather stereotyped thinking.

## Personalised learning

Effective teaching of young people who are gifted but who also have learning difficulties depends particularly on knowing the strengths and weaknesses of individual pupils. Engaging in discussions with people who know a particular pupil well such as parents, the SENCO and members of the pastoral team are important. It is often the case that through such discussions teachers gain a unique insight into pupils making personalised learning a much more realistic goal.

## The school library and external agencies

In order to support children that are gifted in RE, a well-structured religious section in a school library can be a real asset. The internet is also obviously a valuable resource. However, the book is not dead and pupils should be encouraged to make use of the school library when undertaking homework or special assignments. As well as formally using the library to research a topic the joys of serendipity are not to be dismissed. The happy chance of scanning across a line of books, or stumbling across something while flicking through a book, has stirred the passion and energy of young minds in the past and, given the opportunity, is likely to do so again in the future.

Often religious sections in school libraries can look like a fairly sorry assortment. In the section marked 'religion' there may be little more than some Bibles, some children's Bible stories, a few books on world religions and material on myths and legends. Often due to the peculiarities of the Dewey system, books suggested by teachers of RE may appear in other sections of the library under biography, history, travel, art or architecture. Usually school librarians can be persuaded to reclassify books. This ensures that the efforts of a teacher of RE to create a religious section which gives the subject some status may in time be achieved, and that books are not dissipated to sections of the library which a young person interested in religion might not think to visit.

### External agencies

Religious education is a rather narrowly evolved creature which only really survives in schools. Religion, of course, goes on in all sorts of places including places of worship. However, unlike tennis, athletics or drama, there is not a national network of RE clubs which exist outside of schools equivalent to tennis, athletics or drama clubs. A young person that wished to pursue the subject outside school and link up with like-minded people might struggle to find anything which quite meets their needs. There are, of course, church youth clubs, mosque schools and Buddhist meditation centres, for example, which may interest a young person. They may well provide an environment in which thoughtful and informed discussion about religion takes place. However, usually education is not the primary goal of such organisations. Rather they are places in which faith is being nurtured.

Some places of worship both organise and host public talks, discussion groups and lectures which have a religious theme. In the main the targeted audience is adult but that does not mean that a very able young person could not gain a great deal from attending such an event.

## Museums and exhibitions

There are a few permanent exhibitions, which have a specialist religious theme, for example, The Jewish Museum in Camden Town and Finchley, the 'Islamic Exhibition' in Birmingham and the Guru Nanak Sikh Museum in Leicester. The Victoria and Albert Museum has a permanent exhibition in their Asian Galleries exploring the development particularly of Hinduism and Buddhism over thousands of years. Art galleries and museums sometimes stage exhibitions which have a special religious theme. For example, the National Gallery in the summer of 2005 mounted an exhibition of Rembrandt's 'Late Religious Portraits'. The Ashmolean Museum in Oxford is establishing an Inter-Faith Exhibition with the intention of staging special exhibitions with themes like 'Pilgrimage – the Sacred Journey'. These exhibitions can ignite the imagination of young people. However, visitors to such exhibitions often may gain a greater appreciation of art rather than specific insights into religion. It is quite possible that very able young people might be more interested in, and raise more fundamental questions about, life and our place in the universe following a visit to the National Space Centre in Leicester.

## NAGTY Outreach programme and YG&T learner catalogue

For the past five years the National Academy for Gifted and Talented Youth (NAGTY) has provided Outreach programmes for young people who are very able in RE. These have been delivered by experts usually as one-day or up to five-day courses at various locations across the country. To raise the level of challenge they have often had a large philosophical element with topic titles like 'Religion and Philosophy – What is 'Truth'?, 'Philosophy – The Big Questions'. These courses have provided an opportunity for young people to think about questions like 'What is a person?' and 'Can reason alone prove that God exists?'

However, the NAGTY programme has now come to an end and G&T provision is being taken over by CfBT Education Trust who will manage the Young, Gifted and Talented (YG&T) programme. The intention of YG&T is to provide a new 'learner catalogue' which will list online modules, face-to-face courses and other provisions for gifted and talented young people, as well as courses for teachers. At the time of writing this learner catalogue is still being developed but the expectation is that it will contain material which will be of interest to young people gifted in RE.

## Teaching assistants and mentoring

### Teaching assistants

It cannot have escaped the attention of most teachers of RE that over the last five years or so there has been a real increase in the amount of adult support available in the classroom. Usually this adult support is in the form of trained teaching assistants (TA). Many TAs have a brief to support a particular child or group of children that have special needs. However, many TAs are interested and willing to develop their skills. Many, if asked, are prepared to work with a very able child or a group of very able children in order to develop their learning. Of course, it is also possible that a child that has special needs and has been identified for TA support may also be gifted in RE.

A TA may have first-hand knowledge about a particular faith or issue which can be used as an asset and put to good use by asking them to undertake some work with young people in a class that are gifted in RE. For example a TA may have first-hand knowledge of:

- 'arranged marriage' within the Hindu tradition

- key ideas expressed in Gospel songs popular in the Pentecostal Church

- the experience of visiting the Golden Temple in Amritsa

- nursing an elderly patient that has Alzheimer's

- a relative's near-death experience

- Id-ul-Fitr celebrations in a Muslim home

- Bono's views about religion expressed in his biography and songwriting

- growing up as a member of the Christadelphian Church.

However, if a TA is to provide effective support for a very able child or group of very able children in RE, this cannot be some sort of improvised arrangement. A teacher of RE needs to put in some deliberate planning time with the TA well before the lesson begins. A professional dialogue has to take place between the teacher of RE and the TA so that the TA is clear about who they will be working with, what the aim of the lesson is, what strategies they might use, what activities or tasks the pupils might undertake and what resources are available.

## Learning mentors

Learning mentors are employed to work with pupils over a wide range of ability, including the very able. The idea is that a learning mentor will arrange to meet with pupils usually on a one-to-one basis, although group work, after-school clubs and drop-in sessions are all possibilities.

The role of the learning mentor is to target pupils who are underachieving and help them overcome any barrier to learning that is preventing them from learning as effectively as they might. A child that is gifted in RE may well be doing well compared to many but nevertheless may have started to fall behind and be underachieving given the child's real potential. Such pupils should be identified. If a learning mentor is available within the school, making use of them could make a real difference in helping the child to make the progress that they should be achieving. The learning mentor may uncover barriers to learning like difficulties at home, bullying, emotional depression due to the breakdown of an intimate friendship, and may be able to help the pupil address their problem.

## Department mentoring

If a learning mentor is not available within a school, an RE department may wish to instigate its own learning mentoring scheme using members of the department. Very able pupils may be seen on a regular basis to discuss their progress and their response to the work they are doing in RE. Very able children are often able to identify aspects of the subject which interest them the most and which they would like to pursue. Or an able child who is given a voice may identify aspects of RE which they find unappealing or lacking in challenge. Mentoring is not, however, simply a chance for a young person to sound off. Through mentoring a teacher may gain insights into ways in which their teaching is being effective. Alternatively, they may more honestly reflect on their teaching and come to realise that there are indeed ways in which they could be doing a better job.

## Peer mentoring

Some schools, most notably in the London Borough of Camden, have successfully used peer mentoring. This involves identifying able Year 10 students involved in taking an RE GCSE, full or short course, who are underachieving. Identification may be based on noting those students who achieved a very high average point score (APS) at the end of Year 9 and yet, a year or so later, their estimated RE GCSE grades based on mock exams are low.

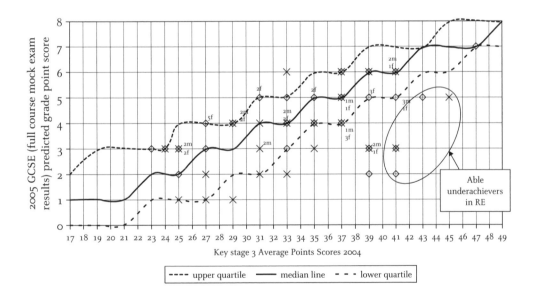

These underachieving students are mentored by students only a few years older than themselves who are now studying at a local college of higher education. Obviously, as with any form of mentoring, appropriate child protection measures have to be in place. That said, the advice and support from peer mentors who are of a similar age and social background and who understand the experiences a young person may be going through, as they may well have experienced something similar themselves, has proved to be very effective.

## Summary

- Being gifted in RE and having learning difficulties is not a contradiction.
- Analyse a pupil's unique learning difficulties in order to make personalised learning a more realistic goal.
- Make use of in-house resources and expertise, TAs, SENCOs, parents.
- Make use of external agencies.
- Introduce a mentoring programme.

# Beyond the classroom

- Gaining the respect of colleagues
- Getting the most out of visits
- RE competitions
- Summer schools
- RE clubs and masterclasses
- Links with experts, FE colleges and universities

The great majority of RE departments that are successful in providing for their very able children enthusiastically provide out-of-classroom activities. Although the primary responsibility is to ensure that effective support for very able pupils is embedded in the mainstream classroom, additional activities beyond the classroom are a highly desirable bonus.

## Gaining the respect of colleagues

Of course, as tag-on extras, there is always the difficulty that out-of-school activities are unlikely to be sustained. They become little more than mere events which are of dubious educational value. However, the truth is that RE in many schools is something of a 'Cinderella' subject that is not properly understood. Some teachers not involved in teaching RE, including members of senior management teams, have little understanding of or regard for the subject. They believe its agenda, whether consciously stated or not, is to serve as an advocate for religion. Its intention is to affirm the values of faith and so implicitly urge faith upon young people. For this reason, they believe the subject is not an honest, academic exploration, and so it fails to command their respect.

As long as RE is only taught in classrooms behind closed doors, there will always be the suspicion that these views are justified. One of the major ways in which an RE department can get across the message that its aims are educational and that it is not a missionary wing of the Church, or of religion in general, is by staging events outside the classroom. Such events give RE a public forum through which it can raise its profile, correct misconceptions and win the respect of colleagues who tend to view the subject in an unfavourable light.

## Getting the most out of visits

The visit, particularly to a local place of worship such as a church, mosque, gurdwara, etc., has long been recognised as of immense educational value. Some local authorities, in their agreed syllabus, make it clear that visiting a place of worship should be an educational entitlement available to all young people in a school. In *The Non-Statutory National Framework for Religious Education* visiting a place of religious significance is stated in the 'Breadth of study' section under the heading, 'Experiences and opportunities'

The benefits of taking young people on visits to a place of worship include the following:

- it brings alive the reality of religious faith and belief in the local community

- it enables young people to learn about a faith at first hand

- it provides a highly memorable educational experience which may help to develop social understanding and counter prejudice.

### A friendly tour

However, although many places of worship welcome visits from local schools, very few of them are really geared up to ensure that a visit from a party of school children is of maximum educational benefit. Often such visits are little more than a friendly tour provided by a leader of the faith community around the building with the emphasis on the furniture, symbols, art and architecture. This is often followed by a talk about the faith's main beliefs or ceremonies and a response to pupils' frequently asked questions.

It is true that such visits are often valuable in that pupils learn to appreciate that people in the places of worship are often friendly, welcoming and very hospitable. However, as a learning experience pupils may be shown so many different items or areas and may have been told so many bits of information that they may fail to retain much, other than a general impression.

All young people, including very able young people are likely to benefit more from visits which have a clearly defined educational goal and where learning outcomes are more clearly agreed.

### A themed visit

A much more challenging and enriched learning experience can be achieved if the teacher plans a themed visit. A themed visit involves focusing on only one aspect of the faith and during the visit exploring that one aspect of the faith in some depth. For example, a mosque visit need not be a rather superficial introduction to all of the Five Pillars of Islam. Instead, the guide might focus only on the meaning, purpose and significance of one of the pillars, perhaps the salah. A visit to a church might have only one theme – the beliefs, views and spiritual rewards of receiving Holy Communion. To be successful a themed visit must be agreed and planned with the member of the community that will act as the main host.

## A planned assignment

A 'planned assignment' involves allocating to pupils, either working individually or in pairs, particular assignments which they are required to undertake in the course of the visit. For example, a very able child might be given a tape recorder or a handheld digital camcorder and be asked to produce a sound diary, or a sound and picture diary, recording their response to what they see or learn during the visit.

Alternatively, they may be asked to interview for ten to fifteen minutes the leader of the place of worship, or a member of the congregation, in order to ask them about their own spiritual journey in life and how their faith has developed and perhaps changed. Or again, a pair of pupils may be given a particular assignment to record what members of the congregation say in response to the question, 'Must a Christian believe in hell?' or 'Does Hinduism teach that there is one God or many gods?' A pupil may be asked to write up the interview, providing an analysis of the different views, in the form of an article for a neighbourhood magazine.

As well as visits to local places of worship, more ambitious visits can prove to be even more fruitful. A large number of cathedrals, for example, Lichfield, Coventry, Canterbury and York Minster all have educational officers. These cathedrals have extensive experience and resources to ensure that a visit is memorable but also highly challenging. Many of these cathedrals, as well as offering general opportunities to learn more about the Christian faith or Christian symbolism, specialise in topics often associated with the building. For example, Canterbury Cathedral provides an RE focus on 'Saints and Martyrs of our Own Time', Coventry Cathedral specialises in 'Conflict and Reconciliation'. At York Minster young people may consider the issues and tension arising from the question, 'York Minster – a place of worship or a tourist attraction?'

## Places of religious significance

Teachers of RE need not confine themselves only to visits to places of worship. Visits can be organised which involve taking pupils to places which are of religious significance rather than places of worship, for example, the Beth Shalom Holocaust Centre, the Imperial War Museum, Glastonbury Abbey or the Shrine of Our Lady of Walsingham. Such trips should not be a repetition of what the history department might organise. Instead an RE visit may be specifically designed to raise different sorts of religious and philosophical questions; for example, 'Why is there evil in the world?' 'Is war ever justified?' 'How did faith survive in the trenches?' 'Did Christians resist Hitler?' 'Was God in the extermination camps?' Both Glastonbury and Walsingham have educational specialists, indeed Glastonbury Abbey has an actor in role as a sixteenth-century monk. These centres are able to arrange programmes on themes like 'Myths and Legends', 'What is a Saint?' 'Pilgrimage as a personal experience' and 'The Big Questions!'

## Educational visits further afield

An RE department might consider organising educational visits outside Great Britain. Study tours to countries like Morocco, Tunisia, Israel and France enable pupils to experience religious life in other cultures and to develop a much more informed understanding of particular religious issues and questions. However, simply observing religion being practised at a well-known location like the Western Wall, the great courtyard mosque at Tunis, or at Taizé, may well be a fascinating experience but it does not in itself guarantee a stimulating educational outcome. While allowing young people to dwell on and take in the experience, activities to accompany such occasions do need to be planned carefully to ensure that pupils are effectively challenged and encouraged to think. Poor questioning or assignment setting like asking pupils to 'Sketch the Mihrab' or 'Find out when the dome was built' do not become stimulating activities simply because they are asked of pupils in a famous location.

Depending of course on where pupils are taken, study tours abroad lend themselves to raising challenging questions like:

- Are holy places created by humans or by God?

- What, if anything, does a religious experience prove?

- What role does the void play in Mosque design?

- Can two religions disagree but both be true?

- Why do differences exist within religions?

- In what way might a large gathering of members of a religion have an impact on their faith?

- What should a person who has a faith be doing about those who practise militant extremism in the name of their faith?

The residential nature of such educational visits can also be a rewarding part of the total experience. Both students and teaching staff learn a great deal about each other as they spend much longer periods of time together. Barriers may break down, quiet personalities may come out of their shells and relationships can develop so that quite a strong sense of bonding in the group may occur. This sense of bonding, as well as having potential dangers, can also result in a number of educational rewards. For example, during residential trips:

- young people may open up enabling them to articulate their ideas and views more carefully and in much more detail than might ever have been achieved in the confines of the classroom

- young people may also show a greater willingness to listen more carefully to what others have to say so that the level of reciprocal dialogue and interactive learning is greatly increased

- it may be possible for very difficult and demanding topics or issues to be discussed at a much greater depth and to be revisited several times potentially resulting in a very intense learning experience.

## RE competitions

There are from time to time a limited number of opportunities for pupils gifted in RE to demonstrate their skills in a competitive forum. For example, the National Association of Teachers of Religious Education (NATRE, formerly Professional Council for RE) together with the services of RE Today have organised a number of national RE competitions.

In 2004 young people submitted art work in a competition called 'Spirited Arts'. The competition inspired artwork on themes like 'The Soul Within', 'Hopes for the future', 'Love in our world' and 'Gautama's four sights'. Entries, including of course, the winning entries were featured in a glossy RE Today Services publication (Barker 2005) and may also be seen online on NATRE's website (www.natre.org.uk).

In 2005 a similar national competition was launched called 'Spirited Poetry'. Entrants were encouraged to express their own thoughts or ideas on religious or spiritual matters through the medium of poetry. If they found it helpful, it was suggested that young people might take as their inspiration various leads such as:

- 'Life's like . . .'

- 'I wonder . . .'

- 'Faith'

- 'Where is God?'

Welcome though these competitions have been, they do tend to be one-off events which are not repeated. Winning entries, and perhaps this reflects the nature of the entries generally, are often very sympathetic towards religious faith. They tend not to have a critical edge, or reflect the maturity of self-scrutiny or doubt, which may also be seen in work produced by the very able. It may be the case that some very able young people believe these competitions have certain expectations. They perhaps imagine that the judges expect to see a sort of religious and moral compliance reflecting polite mainstream views about faith and so produce work to match these expectations.

## Templeton Awards for Religion and Science

An exception to having one-off competitions have been the Templeton Awards for Religion and Science. This competition was also run by RE Today Services with the support of the Templeton Foundation. The competition encouraged young people to think about the nature and possible relationship between science and religion. By engaging in the competition young people often found themselves grappling with concepts like 'materialism', 'spirituality', 'proof' and 'faith'.

## Local authority competitions

Some local authorities, usually with the help of their local SACREs, have attempted to encourage and reward high standards in RE by running competitions in their own authority. Competitions may take different forms, for example, competitors may be asked to submit an essay or produce on a CD a documentary based on a religious theme. Such competitions have resulted in outstanding material being submitted. However, these competitions tend also to be one-off events and limited to only schools within the education authority.

## The West Midlands RE Quiz

One exception to this has been the annual 'RE Quiz' for Key Stage 3 students which has been successfully running in the West Midlands since 2001. Schools from five different authorities enter the competition. Each school has a team of four young people. The overall winners of the quiz, and indeed schools which come in second, third, fourth and fifth, get to keep for a year a quite impressive trophy.

It has to be said that success in the quiz requires an accurate and substantial ability to recall knowledge about the various principal religious traditions. It most certainly is not a quiz which draws from young people their ability to evaluate, empathise or demonstrate how they have learnt from religion. Nevertheless, it is the case that many of the most gifted young people in RE in a school often end up as members of the team. Some of the schools that have regularly entered the competition find that having an RE trophy to put into the school's display cabinet gives the subject a good deal of prestige within the school. It also gives rise each year to a healthy competitive edge amongst young people of ability who want to represent the school in the quiz.

## Summer schools

Since funding has been available for summer schools for gifted and talented pupils, they have tended to range through a diverse collection of different skills and topics. Young people, for example, have found themselves developing their ICT skills, visiting an interactive science museum, making a 'movie', developing their skills as story tellers or programming a robot.

In other words gifted and talented summer schools have provided an opportunity to look at a variety of subjects and topics which it was thought would interest and challenge very able young people. Relatively few gifted and talented summer schools have focused specifically on only one curriculum area, such as RE. Some summer schools have included an RE element such as a trip to a place of religious significance. More frequently, an issue which has a moral dimension to it has been undertaken, for example, pupils might spend an afternoon filming a documentary on an issue like bullying, crime or pollution.

## 'Mind and Muscle' summer school

DialogueWorks, which promotes philosophy for children and reflective thinking, runs a summer school called 'Mind and Muscle'. This summer school combines outdoor activities like kayaking, archery, rock climbing and orienteering with reflection and discussion on issues like honesty, respect, friendship and fairness. Concepts central to the teaching of PSHE, citizenship, moral education and to some extent RE form part of the general enquiry.

## RE clubs and masterclasses

### RE clubs

Although there is a tradition of lunchtime and after-school RE clubs these have always been open to young people of all levels of ability. Often RE clubs have not had as their aim an intense and rigorous extension or enrichment of learning. In many cases they have been very relaxed occasions providing opportunities for club members to:

● chat over issues with the teacher or with other club members

● undertake art or craft work which arose out of the RE lesson, e.g. 'Miss, can we come in at lunchtime and do some more work on our Hindu Shrine?'

● prepare or rehearse a presentation for an RE lesson or for a school assembly

● engage in private research relating to faith or religion.

Perhaps unintentionally in some cases 'RE clubs' have blurred into something resembling Christian Bible classes. Non-members may view such clubs as Christian cliques which provide opportunities for members to explore issues concerning church, faith and the Bible. If religions other than Christianity are mentioned these are sometimes presented as allies in a battle against materialism and secularism. Valuable though clubs of this kind may be for building up good relationships and affirming faith, they cannot be claimed to be suitable additional provision for young people who are gifted in RE.

However, this is not always an accurate picture of many RE clubs. Some RE clubs are very inclusive, welcoming pupils of all ability and of all faiths and also encouraging the involvement of pupils who have no affirmed faith but who may in fact be very sceptical. An RE club may be organised so that there are regular opportunities for young people to bring up topical and also long-standing issues of a religious nature and rigorously explore such issues with others. Sometimes the pupils may provide a presentation to the other club members of subject matter they have taken an interest in and have researched. Or sometimes the teacher may take a lead role, or perhaps a visiting speaker may be invited to speak to the club members, not unlike the way in which a lesson in normal school hours may be organised.

An RE club can provide valuable additional gifted and talented provision. However:

- they are bolt-on extras and require a great deal of will and commitment in order for them to be sustained.

- as they are free and open to all, whether or not young people who are gifted in RE choose to attend is always uncertain. Those very able pupils that do attend often do so because they are highly motivated. The converse, of course, is also true and that is that young people who are gifted in RE but are not motivated are unlikely to attend the club.

- funding sources for an RE club are often limited. Many RE clubs are run by teachers as an act of goodwill and they are not financially reimbursed in any way.

## Philosophy clubs

With the growth of the 'Philosophy for Children' movement (P4C), promoted in Britain particularly by SAPERE and DialogueWorks, philosophy clubs are becoming increasingly popular. A philosophy club may discuss many different issues including topical news items, education, politics, citizenship and aesthetics. However, many issues discussed in a philosophy club could very easily directly link with those covered in RE lessons. For example, issues discussed may include:

- How do we know something is true?

- Does life have a purpose?

- What does it mean to be fully human?

- How do we know right from wrong?

- Do we have free will?

- Does God exist?

- Is there such a thing as a just war?

- Is an embryo a person?

- Why is there evil in the world?

- Is capital punishment wrong?

One of the most important strategies promoted by the 'Philosophy for Children' movement is community of enquiry (see Chapter 5). This strategy encourages pupils themselves to raise questions which they wish to discuss. The direction the discussion takes is also largely in the hands of the pupils themselves. The teacher may seek to influence the topic to be discussed by the choice of stimulus. Or a teacher may attempt to give direction to the discussion itself by asking questions such as 'What do you mean?' 'Can you give an example?' or 'Is there another point of view?' However, in essence it is the children themselves that exercise the greatest influence on what they get to think and talk about.

Philosophy clubs run in this way can be highly stimulating, very challenging and extremely rewarding. Because of this some see a philosophy club using a community of enquiry approach as making a very valuable contribution to pupils' critical thinking particularly in a field like RE where so many of the issues discussed may be of a religious or an ethical nature. Indeed for many teachers such a club is seen as a more acceptable way of providing challenging RE outside of normal school hours rather than adopting a masterclass format. The advantages of such a philosophy club are:

- It is open to all so that pupils self-select whether to be members or not. This removes the selective elitist element associated with masterclasses which many teachers are uncomfortable with.

- The teacher is primarily a facilitator and is not a 'sage on the stage' disseminating their knowledge to largely passive recipients. This results in pupils being much more actively engaged in the learning process and so adopts an approach which is likely to lead to more effective learning.

- Some teachers report that a philosophy club re-engaged very able but disaffected boys who were underachieving in RE. A philosophy club with its emphasis on discussion and avoidance of books, worksheets or writing had a special appeal for boys. Also doing 'philosophy' was seen by boys as being 'cool' whereas RE was often seen, in spite of appeals to the contrary, as being semi-coercive, and so irksome.

A philosophy club does not have to pursue relentlessly the single strategy of community of enquiry. During a philosophy club, young people may play a dilemma game and discover that principles can collide or that choices may have unexpected outcomes. Or pupils may be taught the Socratic technique of asking what a word like 'soul', 'justice' or 'holy' means and testing the definition against possible exceptions.

## Masterclasses

Masterclasses in RE are a series of lessons which take place outside of normal school hours usually after school or perhaps on a Saturday morning. A masterclass is traditionally led by an expert in the field. It is pitched at an intentionally high level and intended only for those young people who are very able in RE.

Masterclasses are often criticised as being elitist in that they exclude young people who are not very able. Some forms of masterclass provision attempt to overcome this problem by making the masterclass available to all and not limiting it only to students on a gifted or talented register. However, in the criteria or information accompanying the classes it is made clear that the lesson or lessons are intended for the very able. In this way those pupils that are less able self-select and choose not to attend.

Another criticism of masterclasses is that they provide provision only to those very able young people that are motivated and are prepared to give up their extra time to attend such classes. Or, in a related criticism, masterclasses are said to favour young people that have aspirational, middle class parents who encourage their children to attend, are able to pay any fee that may be incurred and are more able to overcome transport difficulties as they are more likely to own a car. However, not all very able young people are highly motivated. Some young people find that they have responsibilities at home which they cannot avoid, perhaps as a carer of a parent or of younger siblings. However motivated or able they may be, it is unrealistic for them to attend a masterclass.

Even though they may have weaknesses, masterclasses can offer very real advantages. For example, they can provide:

- an unrivalled, rigorous transmission of information

- a growth in awareness of the methods and techniques used by experts and pioneers in the field of knowledge

- an insight into some of the issues and questions which are part of the contemporary discussion of experts in the field so young people become aware of the issues which lie at the frontiers of knowledge.

Usually the basis of a masterclass is for an expert to guide young people, pursuing in some depth a topic over a lesson or perhaps several lessons. So for example, masterclasses might be organised around topics such as:

- Muhammad and the concept of Prophethood in Islam

- the doctrine of Atonement in Christianity

- the Buddha – what did he teach?

- Plato and his influence on religious thought

- Jewish mysticism – what is it all about?

- Christian Ethical Theory – how do we know right from wrong?

- are all religions the same? A Hindu perspective

- Schleiermacher – The Father of Modern Protestant Theology

- science and learning in Islam.

However there is no need for masterclasses to be planned in the mould of the BBC's Reith Lectures which favour those with good listening skills. A masterclass in RE could be very visual, highly kinaesthetic and actively engage students not unlike The Royal Institution of Great Britain's 'Christmas lectures' which in the tradition of Michael Faraday are full of bangs, crashes and bumps.

As with all out-of-school activities funding can be a problem. One possible solution to this might be the additional funding for personalised learning which has been made available to schools. Within the Dedicated Schools Grant, schools are receiving additional funding to support three areas:

- to provide additional support for pupils who have fallen behind age-related expectations, especially in English and mathematics

- to fund provision for gifted and talented children

- to help children from deprived families to access after-school and year-round activities through the development of extended schools.

## Links with experts, FE colleges and universities

Apart from finance another difficulty with masterclasses is finding suitable experts. One possible solution is for schools to find experts within their local community, perhaps in universities and colleges of further education, in faith communities or by networking with other schools. Individuals with hidden expertise can often be found within a school, or in neighbouring schools, who have both the skills and the knowledge to deliver high quality lessons in a specialist area of RE. For example, within a neighbouring school's science department there may be a teacher that has taken an interest in the debate in America about 'Intelligent design versus Evolutionary theory'. Such expertise could easily provide the basis for a series of highly challenging lessons. Or a local minister may have expert knowledge of 'The theology of John's Gospel' and would enjoy teaching a select group of very able students who are interested in the early development of Christian thinking. Similarly, three secondary schools might identify their most able RE students at the end of Key Stage 3. These students might be offered the opportunity to attend a local college of further education for a weekly afternoon lesson delivered by a member of the college staff. The students would be prepared for possible early entry into a Religious Studies AS exam at the end of Year 11.

## Summary

- Raise the profile of RE within the school.
- Plan visits which have a clearly defined educational goal.
- Encourage a healthy competitive edge to do your best.
- Develop self-confidence in pupils.
- Enable young people of ability to mix with and learn from young people of similar ability.
- Be alert to individuals with hidden expertise that may be used in a teaching role.

# Appendices

Appendix 1.1   Institutional quality standards in gifted and talented education

# Institutional quality standards in gifted and talented education

| Generic Elements | Entry | Developing | Exemplary |
|---|---|---|---|
| | | A – Effective teaching and learning strategies | |
| 1. Identification | i. The school/college has learning conditions and systems to identify gifted and talented pupils in all year groups and an agreed definition and shared understanding of the meaning of 'gifted and talented' within its own, local and national contexts. | i. Individual pupils are screened annually against clear criteria at school/college and subject/topic level. | i. **Multiple criteria and sources of evidence** are used to identify gifts and talents, including through the use of a broad range of quantitative and qualitative data. |
| | ii. An **accurate record** of the identified gifted and talented population is kept and updated. | ii. The record is used to identify under-achievement and **exceptional achievement** (both within and outside the population) and to track/review pupil **progress.** | ii. The record is supported by a comprehensive monitoring, progress planning and reporting system which all staff regularly share and contribute to. |
| | iii. The identified gifted and talented population broadly reflects the school/college's **social and economic composition,** gender and ethnicity. | iii. **Identification** systems address issues of **multiple exceptionality** (pupils with specific gifts/talents and special educational needs). | iii. Identification processes are regularly reviewed and refreshed in the light of pupil performance and value-added data. The gifted and talented population is fully representative of the school/college's population. |
| **Evidence** | | | |
| **Next steps** | | | |
| 2. Effective provision in the classroom | i. The school/college addresses the different needs of the gifted and talented population by providing a stimulating learning environment and by extending the teaching repertoire. | i. Teaching and learning strategies are diverse and flexible, meeting the needs of distinct pupil groups within the gifted and talented population (e.g. able underachievers, exceptionally able). | i. The school/college has established a range of methods to find out what works best in the classroom, and shares this within the school/college and with other schools and colleges. |
| | ii. Teaching and learning is differentiated and delivered through both individual and group activities. | ii. A range of challenging learning and teaching strategies is evident in lesson planning and delivery. **Independent learning** skills are developed. | ii. Teaching and learning are suitably challenging and varied, incorporating the breadth, depth and pace required to progress high achievement. Pupils routinely work independently and self-reliantly. |

| | | | |
|---|---|---|---|
| | iii. Opportunities exist to extend learning through **new technologies**. | iii. The use of **new technologies** across the curriculum is focused on **personalised learning** needs. | iii. The innovative use of new technologies raises the achievement and motivation of gifted and talented pupils. |
| Evidence | | | |
| Next steps | | | |
| 3. Standards | i. Levels of **attainment** and **achievement** for gifted and talented pupils are comparatively high in relation to the rest of the school/college population and are in line with those of similar pupils in similar schools/colleges. | i. Levels of **attainment** and **achievement** for gifted and talented pupils are broadly consistent across the gifted and talented population and above those of similar pupils in similar schools/colleges. | i. Levels of attainment and achievement for gifted and talented pupils indicate sustainability over time and are well above those of similar pupils in similar schools/colleges. |
| | ii. Self-evaluation indicates that gifted and talented provision is satisfactory. | ii. Self-evaluation indicates that gifted and talented provision is good. | ii. Self-evaluation indicates that gifted and talented provision is very good or excellent. |
| | iii. Schools/colleges' gifted and talented education programmes are explicitly linked to the achievement of SMART outcomes and these highlight improvements in pupils' attainment and achievement. | | |
| Evidence | | | |
| Next steps | | | |

## B – Enabling curriculum entitlement and choice

| | | | |
|---|---|---|---|
| 4. Enabling curriculum entitlement and choice | i. Curriculum organisation is flexible, with opportunities for enrichment and increasing subject/topic choice. Pupils are provided with support and guidance in making choices. | i. The curriculum offers opportunities and guidance to pupils which enable them to work beyond their age and/or phase, and across subjects or topics, according to their aptitudes and interests. | i. The curriculum offers personalised learning pathways for pupils which maximise individual potential, retain flexibility of future choices, extend well beyond test/examination requirements and result in sustained impact on pupil attainment and achievement. |
| Evidence | | | |
| Next steps | | | |

Definitions for words and phrases in bold are provided in the glossary in the Quality Standards *User Guide*, available at www2.teachernet.gov.uk/gat. QS Model October 2005

| Generic Elements | Entry | Developing | Exemplary |
|---|---|---|---|
| **C – Assessment for learning** | | | |
| 5. Assessment for learning | i. Processes of data analysis and pupil assessment are employed throughout the school/college to plan learning for gifted and talented pupils. | i. Routine progress reviews, using both qualitative and quantitative data, make effective use of prior, predictive and value-added attainment data to plan for progression in pupils' learning. | i. Assessment data are used by teachers and across the school/college to ensure challenge and sustained progression in individual pupils' learning. |
| | ii. Dialogue with pupils provides focused feedback which is used to plan future learning. | ii. Systematic oral and written feedback helps pupils to set challenging curricular targets. | ii. Formative assessment and individual target setting combine to maximise and celebrate pupils' achievements. |
| | iii. Self and peer assessment, based on clear understanding of criteria, are used to increase pupils' responsibility for learning. | iii. Pupils reflect on their own skill development and are involved in the design of their own targets and tasks. | iii. Classroom practice regularly requires pupils to reflect on their own progress against targets, and engage in the direction of their own learning. |
| Evidence | | | |
| Next steps | | | |
| 6. Transfer and transition | i. Shared processes, using agreed criteria, are in place to ensure the productive transfer of information from one setting to another (i.e. from class to class, year to year and school/college to school/college). | i. Transfer information concerning gifted and talented pupils, including parental input, informs targets for pupils to ensure progress in learning. Particular attention is given to including new admissions. | i. Transfer data concerning gifted and talented pupils are used to inform planning of teaching and learning at subject/aspect/topic and individual pupil level, and to ensure progression according to ability rather than age or phase. |
| Evidence | | | |
| Next steps | | | |
| **D – School/college organisation** | | | |
| 7. Leadership | i. A named member of the governing body, senior management team and the lead professional responsible for gifted and talented education have clearly directed responsibilities for motivating and driving gifted and talented provision. The head teacher actively champions gifted and talented provision. | i. Responsibility for gifted and talented provision is distributed, and evaluation of its impact shared, at all levels in the school/college. Staff subscribe to policy at all levels. Governors play a significant supportive and evaluative role. | i. Organisational structures, communication channels and the deployment of staff (e.g. workforce remodelling) are flexible and creative in supporting the delivery of personalised learning. Governors take a lead in celebrating achievements of gifted and talented pupils. |
| Evidence | | | |
| Next steps | | | |

| | | | |
|---|---|---|---|
| **8. Policy** | i. The gifted and talented policy is integral to the school/college's inclusion agenda and approach to personalised learning, feeds into and from the single school/college improvement plan and is consistent with other policies. | i. The policy directs and reflects best practice in the school/college, is regularly reviewed and is clearly linked to other policy documentation. | i. The policy includes input from the whole school/college community and is regularly refreshed in the light of innovative national and international practice. |
| **Evidence** | | | |
| **Next steps** | | | |
| **9. School/college ethos and pastoral care** | i. The school/college sets high expectations, recognises achievement and celebrates the successes of all its pupils.<br><br>ii. The school/college identifies and addresses the particular social and emotional needs of gifted and talented pupils in consultation with pupils, parents and carers. | i. The school/college fosters an environment which promotes positive behaviour for learning. Pupils are listened to and their views taken into account.<br><br>ii. Strategies exist to counteract bullying and any adverse effects of social and curriculum pressures. Specific support for able underachievers and pupils from different cultures and social backgrounds is available and accessible. | i. An ethos of ambition and achievement is agreed and shared by the whole school/college community. Success across a wide range of abilities is celebrated.<br><br>ii. The school/college places equal emphasis on high achievement and emotional well being, underpinned by programmes of support personalised to the needs of gifted and talented pupils. There are opportunities for pupils to use their gifts to benefit other pupils and the wider community. |
| **Evidence** | | | |
| **Next steps** | | | |
| **10. Staff development** | i. Staff have received professional development in meeting the needs of gifted and talented pupils. | i. The induction programme for new staff addresses gifted and talented issues, both at whole school/college and specific subject/aspect level. | i. There is ongoing audit of staff needs and an appropriate range of professional development in gifted and talented education. Professional development is informed by research and collaboration within and beyond the school/college. |

Definitions for words and phrases in bold are provided in the glossary in the Quality Standards *User Guide*, available at www2.teachernet.gov.uk/gat. QS Model October 2005
© Crown Copyright 2005–2007.

| Generic Elements | Entry | Developing | Exemplary |
|---|---|---|---|
| | ii. The lead professional responsible for gifted and talented education has received appropriate professional development. | ii. Subject/aspect and phase leaders have received specific professional development in meeting the needs of gifted and talented pupils. | ii. Priorities for the development of gifted and talented provision are included within a professional development entitlement for all staff and are monitored through performance management processes. |
| Evidence | | | |
| Next steps | | | |
| 11. Resources | i. Provision for gifted and talented pupils is supported by appropriate budgets and resources. | i. Allocated resources include school/college based and nationally available resources, and these have a significant and measurable impact on the progress that pupils make and their attitudes to learning. | i. Resources are used to stimulate innovative and experimental practice, which is shared throughout the school/college and which are regularly reviewed for impact and best value. |
| Evidence | | | |
| Next steps | | | |
| 12. Monitoring and evaluation | i. Subject and phase audits focus on the quality of teaching and learning for gifted and talented pupils. Whole school/college targets are set using prior attainment data. | i. Performance against targets (including at pupil level) is regularly reviewed. Targets include qualitative pastoral and curriculum outcomes as well as numerical data. | i. Performance against targets is rigorously evaluated against clear criteria. Qualitative and quantitative outcomes inform whole-school/college self-evaluation processes. |
| | ii. Elements of provision are planned against clear objectives within effective whole-school self-evaluation processes. | ii. All elements, including non-academic aspects of gifted and talented provision, are planned to clear objectives and are subjected to detailed evaluation. | ii. The school/college examines and challenges its own provision to inform development of further experimental and innovative practice in collaboration with other schools/colleges. |
| Evidence | | | |
| Next steps | | | |

## E – Strong partnerships beyond the school

| | Entry | Developing | | | Exemplary |
|---|---|---|---|---|---|
| 13. Engaging with the community, families and beyond | i. Parents/carers are aware of the school's/college's policy on gifted and talented provision, contribute to its identification processes and are kept informed of developments in gifted and talented provision, including through the School Profile. | i. Progression of gifted and talented pupils is enhanced by home-school/college partnerships. There are strategies to engage and support hard-to-reach parents/carers. | | | i. Parents/carers are actively engaged in extending provision. Support for gifted and talented provision is integrated with other children's services (e.g. Sure Start, EAL, traveller, refugee, LAC Services). |
| | ii. The school/college shares good practice and has some collaborative provision with other schools, colleges and the wider community. | ii. A coherent strategy for networking with other schools, colleges and local community organisations extends and enriches provision. | | | ii. There is strong emphasis on collaborative and innovative working with other schools/colleges which impacts on quality of provision locally, regionally and nationally. |
| Evidence | | | | | |
| Next steps | | | | | |
| 14. Learning beyond the classroom | i. There are opportunities for pupils to learn beyond the school/college day and site (extended hours and out-of-school activities). | i. A coherent programme of enrichment and extension activities (through extended hours and out-of-school activities) complements teaching and learning and helps identify pupils' latent gifts and talents. | | | i. Innovative models of learning beyond the classroom are developed in collaboration with local and national schools/colleges to further enhance teaching and learning. |
| | ii. Pupils participate in dedicated gifted and talented activities (e.g. summer schools) and their participation is recorded. | ii. Local and national provision helps meet individual pupils' learning needs, e.g. NAGTY membership, accessing outreach, local enrichment programmes. | | | ii. Coherent strategies are used to direct and develop individual expert performance via external agencies, e.g. HE/FE links, online support, and local/regional/national programmes. |
| Evidence | | | | | |
| Next steps | | | | | |

Definitions for words and phrases in bold are provided in the glossary in the Quality Standards *User Guide*, available at www2.teachernet.gov.uk/gat. QS Model October 2005

© Crown Copyright 2005–2007.

# References

Barker, R. (ed.) (2005) *Spirited Arts: Exploring and expressing through art in secondary RE.* Birmingham: RE Today Services.

Baumfield, V. (2002) *Thinking through Religious Education.* Cambridge: Chris Kington Publishing.

Bloom, B.S. & Krathwohl, D.R. (1956) *Taxonomy of Educational Objectives: The Classification of Educational Goals.* New York: Longman.

Department for Education and Employment (1997) *Excellence in Schools.* London: DfEE.

Department for Education and Skills (DFES) (2002) *Gifted and Talented Provision: An Overview.* London: DfES.

DfES/QCA (2004) *The Non-Statutory National Framework for Religious Education,* QCA/04/1336. London: QCA.

Fisher, R. (1990) *Teaching Children to Think.* London: Stanley Thornes.

Freeman, J. (2001) *Gifted Children Grown Up.* London: David Fulton.

HM Government (2005) *Higher Standards, Better Schools for All.*

Ofsted *Subject Reports 2002/03: Religious Education in Secondary Schools.* HMI.

Ofsted (2003) *Handbook for Inspecting Secondary Schools.* London: Ofsted.

Schools Council (1977) *Occasional Bulletin: A Groundplan for the Study of Religion.* London: Schools Council.

Templeton Foundation (2004) *A Nation Deceived.* http://NationDeceived.org.

Wintersgill, B. (1994) *Ways of Saying.* London: Longman.

Wintersgill, B. (2000) *Task-setting in Religious Education at Key Stage 3 Resource* Issue 22:3. Birmingham: NATRE.

# Further information

## Useful addresses

Guru Nanak Sikh Museum, 9 Holy Bones, Leicester LE1 4LJ
Islamic Exhibition, 434 Coventry Road, Birmingham B10 OUG
Jewish Museum, Camden Town, Raymond Burton House, 129–131 Albert Street,
   London NW1 7NB
Jewish Museum, Finchley, Sternberg Centre, 80 East End Road, London N3 2SY
National Space Centre, Exploration Drive, Leicester LE4 5NS

## Useful websites

www.canterbury-cathedral.org
www.coventrycathedral.org.uk
www.dialogueworks.co.uk
www.lichfield-cathedral.org
www.natre.org.uk
www.ncaction.org.uk
www.retoday.org.uk
www.sapere.org.uk
www.yorkminster.org